# Margaret of Anjou
## Queen of England

# Margaret of Anjou

*Queen of England*

UNIVERSITY OF MIAMI PRESS
Coral Gables, Florida

This translation © 1970 Elek Books Limited
All rights reserved

ISBN 0–87024–214–8
Library of Congress Catalog Card Number: 79-161438

First published in French under the title
MARGUERITE D'ANJOU ET LA GUERRE DES DEUX ROSES
© 1961 Librairie Académique Perrin

Printed in Great Britain by Unwin Brothers Limited,
The Gresham Press, Old Woking, Surrey, England
A member of the Staples Printing Group

*Suffolk*. Be what thou wilt, thou art my prisoner. *Gazes on her*.
  O fairest beauty, do not fear nor fly!
  For I will touch thee but with reverent hands,
  And lay them gently on thy tender side.
  I kiss these fingers for eternal peace.
  Who art thou, say, that I may honour thee?
*Margaret*. Margaret my name, and daughter to a king,
  The King of Naples—whosoe'er thou art.
*Suffolk*. An earl I am, and Suffolk am I call'd.
  Be not offended, nature's miracle,
  Thou art allotted to be ta'en by me:
  So doth the swan her downy cygnets save,
  Keeping them prisoner underneath her wings.
  Yet, if this servile usage once offend,
  Go and be free again as Suffolk's friend. *She is going*.
  O, stay!—I have no power to let her pass;
  My hand would free her, but my heart says no.
  As plays the sun upon the glassy streams,
  Twinkling another counterfeited beam,
  So seems this gorgeous beauty to mine eyes.
  Fain would I woo her, yet I dare not speak:
  I'll call for pen and ink, and write my mind.
  Fie, de la Pole! disable not thyself;
  Hast not a tongue? Is she not prisoner here?
  Wilt thou be daunted at a woman's sight?
  Ay, beauty's princely majesty is such
  Confounds the tongue and makes the senses rough.
*Margaret*. Say, Earl of Suffolk, if thy name be so,
  What ransom must I pay before I pass?
  For I perceive I am thy prisoner.
*Suffolk*. How canst thou tell she will deny thy suit,
  Before thou make a trial of her love?
*Margaret*. Why speak'st thou not? What ransom must I pay?
*Suffolk*. She's beautiful, and therefore to be woo'd;
  She is a woman, therefore to be won.
*Margaret*. Wilt thou accept of ransom, yea or no?

*Suffolk*. Fond man, remember that thou hast a wife;
　Then how can Margaret be thy paramour?
*Margaret*. 'Twere best to leave him, for he will not hear.
*Suffolk*. There all is marr'd; there lies a cooling card.
*Margaret*. He talks at random; sure, the man is mad.
*Suffolk*. And yet a dispensation may be had.
*Margaret*. And yet I would that you would answer me.
*Suffolk*. I'll win this Lady Margaret. For whom?
　Why, for my king! Tush, that's a wooden thing!
*Margaret*. He talks of wood: it is some carpenter.
*Suffolk*. Yet so my fancy may be satisfied,
　And peace established between these realms.
　But there remains a scruple in that too;
　For though her father be the King of Naples,
　Duke of Anjou and Maine, yet is he poor,
　And our nobility will scorn the match.
*Margaret*. Hear ye, captain, are you not at leisure?
*Suffolk*. It shall be so, disdain they ne'er so much;
　Henry is youthful, and will quickly yield.—
　Madam, I have a secret to reveal.
*Margaret*. What though I be enthrall'd? He seems a knight,
　And will not any way dishonour me.
*Suffolk*. Lady, vouchsafe to listen what I say.
*Margaret*. Perhaps I shall be rescu'd by the French;
　And then I need not crave his courtesy.
*Suffolk*. Sweet madam, give me hearing in a cause—
*Margaret*. Tush, women have been captivate ere now.
*Suffolk*. Lady, wherefore talk you so?
*Margaret*. I cry you mercy, 'tis but *quid* for *quo*.
*Suffolk*. Say, gentle Princess, would you not suppose
　Your bondage happy, to be made a queen?
*Margaret*. To be a queen in bondage is more vile
　Than is a slave in base servility;
　For princes should be free.
*Suffolk*. 　　　　　　　　　　　And so shall you,
　If happy England's royal king be free.

*Margaret.* Why, what concerns his freedom unto me?
*Suffolk.* I'll undertake to make thee Henry's queen,
    To put a golden sceptre in thy hand
    And set a precious crown upon thy head,
    If thou wilt condescend to be my—
*Margaret.*                                        What?
*Suffolk.* His love.
*Margaret.* I am unworthy to be Henry's wife.
*Suffolk.* No, gentle madam, I unworthy am
    To woo so fair a dame to be his wife,
    And have no portion in the choice myself.
    How say you, madam, are ye so content?
*Margaret.* And if my father please, I am content.
                   (*Shakespeare: 1 Henry VI, 5.iii*)


*Richard.* Have done thy charm, thou hateful wither'd hag.
*Queen Margaret.* And leave out thee? stay dog, for thou
       shalt hear me.
    If Heaven have any grievous plague in store,
    Exceeding those that I can wish upon thee,
    O let them keep it, till thy sins be ripe,
    And then hurl down their indignation
    On thee, the troubler of the poor world's peace.
    The worm of conscience still begnaw thy soul,
    Thy friends suspect for traitors while thou liv'st,
    And take deep traitors for thy dearest friends:
    No sleep close up that deadly eye of thine,
    Unless it be while some tormenting dream
    Affrights thee with a Hell of ugly devils.
    Thou elvish mark'd, abortive rooting hog,
    Thou that wast seal'd in thy nativity
    The slave of Nature, and the son of Hell:
    Thou slander of thy heavy mother's womb,
    Thou loathed issue of thy father's loins,
    Thou rag of honour, thou detested—
               (*Shakespeare: Richard III, 1.iii*)

# Contents

## BOOK THREE—THE HURRICANE

# Illustrations

# List of Principal Characters

---

## FRANCE

---

**CHARLES VII**
(1403–61) King of France 1422–61, son of the mad Charles VI.

**ISABEAU OF BAVARIA**
Mother of Charles VII.

**MARIE OF ANJOU**
Queen of France, wife of Charles VII. She was the daughter of Yolande of Aragon and sister to René of Anjou.

**LOUIS XI**
(1423–83) Son of Charles VII, he was the Dauphin until 1461 when he succeeded his father as king.

**AGNES SOREL**
Charles VII's mistress.

**GEORGES DE LA TRÉMOILLE**
A favourite of Charles VII.

**PIERRE DE BRÉZÉ**
Senechal of Poitou and friend of Margaret of Anjou.

**RENÉ OF ANJOU**
The father of Margaret. Duke of Lorraine and Bar, Count of Provence, Duke of Anjou, King of Naples and Sicily, he was the son of Louis II of Sicily and Yolande of Aragon, and brother-in-law to Charles VII.

**YOLANDE OF ARAGON**
Wife of Louis II of Anjou and daughter of King John of

Aragon, she was the mother of René of Anjou and of Marie, wife of Charles VII.

MARGARET OF ANJOU
(1430–82) Daughter of René of Anjou, she was married in 1445, at the age of fifteen, to Henry VI of England.

JOHN DUKE OF CALABRIA
Son of René of Anjou and brother to Margaret.

YOLANDE OF ANJOU
Younger daughter of René of Anjou, sister to Margaret, she married Ferry de Vaudémont.

CARDINAL DE BAR
Uncle of René of Anjou.

ISABEL, DUCHESS OF LORRAINE
Wife of René of Anjou, mother of Margaret, she was the daughter of Charles the Bold of Lorraine and Margaret of Bavaria.

LOUIS I OF ANJOU
Brother of Charles V of France. Father of Louis II of Anjou and grandfather of René of Anjou.

LOUIS II OF ANJOU
Father of René of Anjou and husband of Yolande of Aragon.

LOUIS III OF ANJOU
Elder brother of René of Anjou.

CHARLES OF ANJOU
Younger brother of René.

QUEEN JOANNA I OF NAPLES
Adopted René of Anjou and left him the kingdom of Naples.

CHARLES THE BOLD
(1364–1431) Duke of Lorraine, father-in-law of René of Anjou.

# BURGUNDY

**PHILIP THE GOOD**
(d. 1467) Duke of Burgundy, great-grandson of King John II of France.

**CHARLES THE RASH**
(1433–77) Duke of Burgundy, the son of Philip the Good. He was Count of Charolais before succeeding his father as Duke in 1467.

**JOHN OF LUXEMBOURG**
Vassal of Philip the Good, who seized the county of Guise from René of Anjou.

**COUNT OF ST POL**
Brother of John of Luxembourg and Constable of France under Louis XI.

**ANTOINE DE VAUDÉMONT**
Nephew of Charles the Bold of Lorraine, he disputed the succession with René of Anjou after his uncle's death in 1431.

**FERRY DE VAUDÉMONT**
Son of Antoine, married Yolande of Anjou.

## ENGLAND

*Lancastrians*

HENRY VI
King of England, husband of Margaret of Anjou.

HUMPHREY, DUKE OF GLOUCESTER
Protector of England, uncle of Henry VI.

CARDINAL BEAUFORT OF WINCHESTER
Son of John of Gaunt, Duke of Lancaster, and Catherine Swinford. Great-uncle to Henry VI.

WILLIAM DE LA POLE, EARL OF SUFFOLK
Arranged the marriage between Margaret and Henry VI.

LORD SAY
Treasurer, executed by Jack Cade's rebels.

CARDINAL KEMP
Archbishop of Canterbury.

BISHOP OF CHICHESTER
Lord Chancellor.

EDMUND BEAUFORT, SECOND DUKE OF SOMERSET
Descendant of John of Gaunt by his third marriage. Killed at First Battle of St Albans (1455).

HENRY BEAUFORT, THIRD DUKE OF SOMERSET
Eldest son of Edmund, second Duke of Somerset. Executed after Battle of Hexham (1463).

EDMUND BEAUFORT, FOURTH DUKE OF SOMERSET
Second son of Edmund, Second Duke of Somerset. Killed at Battle of Tewkesbury (1471).

EDWARD PRINCE OF WALES
(1453–71) Son of Henry VI and Margaret of Anjou.

SIR JOHN TALBOT
Later Earl of Shrewsbury, English general.

OWEN TUDOR
Married Catherine of Valois, widow of Henry V, and

had two sons, Edmund Earl of Richmond and Jasper. Edmund's son Henry Tudor, was to become Henry VII.

*Yorkists*

RICHARD PLANTAGENET
Duke of York, great-grandson of Edward III.

EDWARD, EARL OF MARCH
Son of Richard, Duke of York, later Edward IV. Married Elizabeth Woodville.

EDMUND, EARL OF RUTLAND
Son of Richard, Duke of York, killed at the battle of Wakefield aged fifteen.

GEORGE, DUKE OF CLARENCE
Son of Richard, Duke of York, married Isabel Neville, daughter of the Earl of Warwick.

RICHARD, DUKE OF GLOUCESTER
Son of Richard, Duke of York, later Richard III. Married Anne Neville, daughter of the Earl of Warwick and widow of Edward of Lancaster the Prince of Wales and son of Henry VI.

MARGARET OF YORK
Daughter of Richard of York, married Charles the Rash, Duke of Burgundy.

RICHARD NEVILLE, EARL OF WARWICK
The Kingmaker, son of the Earl of Salisbury and nephew of Richard of York.

JACK CADE
Irish adventurer who claimed to be Edmund Mortimer, heir to the throne through his descent from the second son of Edward III, and raised a rebellion in Kent.

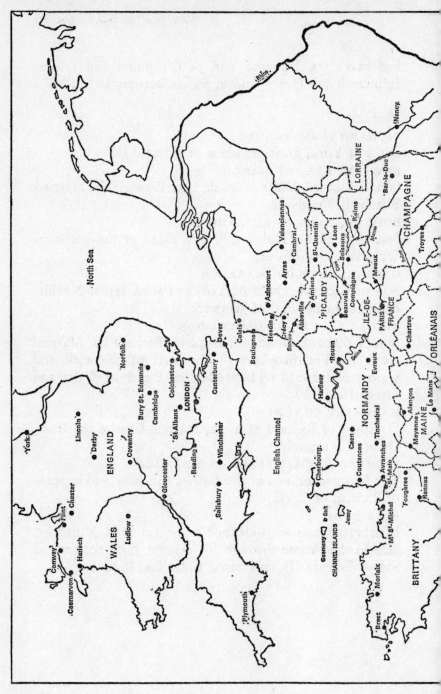

North Sea

York

Lincoln

Derby

ENGLAND

Coventry

Norfolk

Bury St. Edmunds

Cambridge

Colchester

St Albans

LONDON

Canterbury

Dover

Calais

Boulogne

Hesdin

Agincourt

Crécy

Abbeville

Amiens

Arras

Valenciennes

Cambrai

St-Quentin

Laon

Soissons

Compiègne

Beauvais

PICARDY

Reims

Meaux

ILE-DE-

PARIS

FRANCE

Chartres

ORLÉANAIS

Troyes

CHAMPAGNE

Bar-le-Duc

Nancy

LORRAINE

Rhine

Reading

Winchester

Salisbury

Gloucester

Ludlow

WALES

Flint

Chester

Conway

Harlech

Caernarvon

English Channel

Harfleur

Rouen

Evreux

NORMANDY

Caen

Coutances

Cherbourg

Avranches

St-Malo

Mt St-Michel

Fougères

Rennes

BRITTANY

Morlaix

Brest

Tinchebrai

Alençon

Mayenne

MAINE

Le Mans

Guernsey

Jersey

Sark

CHANNEL ISLANDS

Plymouth

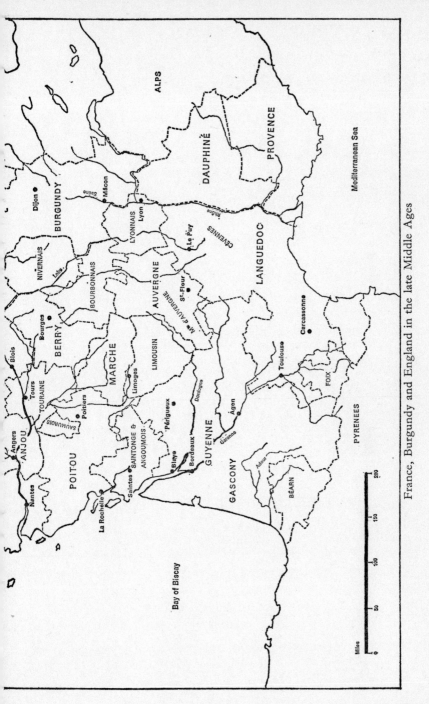

France, Burgundy and England in the late Middle Ages

# Introduction to the English Edition

History is both an art and a science, but history as a science has neither the assurance nor the standing of history as an art, for it is often conjectural and above all it has no absolutes. The same event looks different according to the national points of view of its interpreters or of the teachers expounding it. And legends, more enduring in our memories than the plain reality, may so mask events that they become unrecognizable.

England and France have been fascinated by each other for many centuries. There are few examples of two peoples at once so dissimilar and so dependent upon each other. At times their wars, at other times their alliance have determined the evolution of the Western world and even, indeed, of the whole world. The sea which separates them and which was for so long so difficult to cross, has borne from shore to shore both great ideas and ideals, pure, or mixed with expedients. Hate and love have succeeded each other with the violence, if not the regularity, of the ebb and flow of Channel tides; but even the greatest storms of strong feeling have cast up a fertile alluvium on both Channel coasts.

This immense movement has never had the same aspect from London as from Paris. Until a very recent epoch, history was charged with the mission of exalting nationalist passions, national pride and glory. Today a different school of historians applies itself to a cold study of the facts, to place them in their true light without regard to subjective notions of good and bad ('I am', proclaimed Michelet during the Romantic period, 'for the good and against the wicked.'); the historian now seeks to explore the profound complexity of the play of policies, the souls of princes, without claiming in advance that he will reach a conclusion in favour of this or that country, this or that system.

It is for this reason that little by little, and very happily, the prejudices which made it impossible to understand our neighbours are vanishing. And this change in point of view, a change in the very nature of the historical eye, sometimes serves to reveal the objective truth—in so far as it is capable of being revealed at all.

The Wars of the Roses were a very considerable event in the history of England. A woman whose rôle in that war was decisive was French. Nearly five centuries after her death an impartial Frenchman brought up in his country's traditions but who is a friend and admirer of England, has tried, using modern methods, to review the indictment whereby posterity tried Henry VI's fascinating Queen, and ultimately condemned her.

He will be happy indeed if his work enables the English reader to look with a more understanding and indulgent eye at the woman who—at fifteen years of age!—was charged with the task of wiping the memory of the Hundred Years War from the minds of both English and French.

PHILIPPE ERLANGER
1970

# Introduction

The Hundred Years War—or rather the second Hundred Years War*—between France and England was one of the greatest calamities ever to afflict mankind. Civil war raged as fiercely as the foreign war and to both were added organized brigandage and epidemic disease. The embattled peoples gave free rein to an almost incredible savagery, and conduct declined so far below the civilized level that cannibalism was practised in the very suburbs of Paris. The population of France was reduced by a third and not until the eighteenth century did it recover to the point it attained, on a smaller territory, early in the fourteenth.

The phases of the struggle followed each other in more or less the same order in both countries. And a domestic crisis regularly accompanied every defeat.

From 1340 to 1360 England was victorious, winning the battles of Crécy and Poitiers; following the Treaty of Brétigny she was mistress of one half of John II's kingdom. Domestic reaction was inevitable: Etienne Marcel's†

---

* The first, which broke out over Eleonore of Aquitaine's divorce from Louis VII of France when she left him to marry Henry II of England, lasted from 1152 to 1259. The second, deriving from the Salic Law and Edward III's claim to the French throne, extended from 1337 to 1453.

† Etienne Marcel (1316–1358) was a Paris merchant. He played a large part in the States General of 1355 and 1357, opposing the power of the

first attempt at a bourgeois revolution in Paris; and the atrocious *Jacquerie* uprising of the peasants in the country in 1358.

Charles V overcame these difficulties and thanks to Du Guesclin's military leadership, gave victory to the French; at his death in 1380 the English held only five towns of any consequence on the Continent. But the English, commonly so level-headed and hard working, were drunk on old victories, and now dreamed only of raids, tribute, exemption from taxation. As Michelet put it, 'The rich stock of ill temper with which nature had endowed them was in splendid ferment'.

The young King Richard II, Edward III's successor, was weak, violent and corrupt. Harassed by plots in his own family, and by his Parliament, he had recourse to threatening the great landowning nobles, which was not tolerated. His cousin, Henry of Lancaster, sometimes known as Bolingbroke, was backed by the Church and most of the nobles. Richard II was dethroned, then murdered; Lancaster became King as Henry IV, despite the claims of the Earl of March.

To reinforce his usurped power, Henry IV closely associated the strength of Crown and Church; for, of the nation's 56,000 fiefs, no less than 28,000 belonged to the Church. His son Henry V, after a turbulent youth, might, when he came to the throne in 1413, have 'served as an example even to the clergy.'

This icy-hearted young man, eaten up by an ambition worthy of an Alexander or a Caesar, was determined to distinguish his dynasty with all the fame of the victors of Crécy. His opportunity was the fratricidal strife between the Armagnacs and the Burgundians in a France ruled by the mad Charles VI. Henry landed in France, wiped out

Dauphin Charles (Charles V). He was *prévôt* of the Paris merchants, and tried to force through a constitution. He was assassinated in 1358. The Jacquerie was a peasants' revolt after the French defeat at Poitiers in 1358.

the French nobility at Agincourt in 1415, and subsequently conquered Normandy after a second expedition in 1417. This further aggravated the civil war and John the Fearless, Duke of Burgundy perpetrated an atrocious massacre of Parisians, before losing his own life to the knights of the Dauphin Charles, nominal leader of the Armagnac party. The French queen, Isabeau of Bavaria, who hated her son, and the new Duke of Burgundy, Philip the Good, threw themselves into Henry's arms. Henry married Catherine of Valois, Charles VI's daughter and by the Treaty of Troyes (1420) was recognized heir to the French throne.

It is possible that, had he lived, Henry V might have succeeded in fusing the two nations together and changing the course of history. But he died at the age of thirty-five, a few weeks before Charles VI, in 1422. Thus it was his ten-months-old son, Henry VI, who received the title of King of France and England, while south of the Loire a handful of loyalists hailed the wretched Dauphin as Charles VII of France.

During the next seven years, war dragged on between the two exhausted countries. In London, the child-King's kinsmen were disputing among themselves. Meanwhile, at the court of the 'King of Bourges' there was fierce strife between a faction of unworthy favourites and the 'resistance' party led by Yolande of Aragon, mother of Queen Marie of Anjou.

In 1428 the English made a supreme effort to win a decisive victory by laying siege to Orleans. It was then that Joan of Arc came upon the scene, and victory changed sides again: in twenty-four years England lost all her French possessions excepting Calais. And in doing so she unwittingly laid her future course. Had she been victorious she would have been bound to the European continent and ruled by the Plantagenets, who never lost the stamp of their French origins. Lightened of her Norman, Angevin and Gascon provinces, however, England found herself an island indeed; and turned her attention seaward. The Tudors were to be her first monarchs of British stock.

France, for her part, owed to her reverses her violent emancipation from the vices of regional agressiveness and tyranny. The invader's sword harshly threatened first one and then another part of the country, forced them into union as a 'fatherland', first of its kind in the world, for the word *patrie* came into being with the thing it named. Henry V's undertaking aimed at fusion; it produced the diametrically opposite result. Never did the would-be founder of an empire miss his aim so utterly; never were two peoples so widely separated from each other by an effort to unite them.

Thrown back upon his island, the Englishman left his adversary with a strong government and a sense of national unity. And with the mortification of his defeat he carried home anarchy, discord and even that royal madness which Henry VI inherited from his grandfather Charles VI. There followed the appalling spectacle of a nation given over to hysteria. For thirty years the English spilt each other's blood. The War of the Roses is a pretty name for a hideous dynastic struggle which destroyed countless English people.

This tragedy, which found its celebrant poet in Shakespeare, was not simply the consequence of a military disaster. It resulted also from the fact that 'the wholly artificial fabric of the England of the Middle Ages rested on two matters: on the one hand an infallible and inviolable King who, however, was judged and found wanting in every alternate reign; and, on the other hand, a Church no less inviolable which, being no more than a great aristocratic and territorial establishment using religion as a cloak, was for ever on the verge of being despoiled and ruined. The English carried that genius for legal fiction which the Romans had shown only in civil law, into constitutional law.'*

A remarkable propensity for hair-splitting was, indeed, required, to act out the extraordinary comedy which ten times repeated, ended in the extermination of the Plantagenets.

In normal times everyone pretended to equate king and royalty, monarch and monarchy, the fallible man with the infallible principle. But then, at almost regular intervals, patience was exhausted, the equation was abandoned, and there was bloody strife. Edward II, Richard II, and Henry IV were murdered. Henry II, John Lackland and Henry III humiliated and reduced to impotence.

The fact is that from the end of the twelfth century, nobles and commons had combined to strangle the power of the crown. In 1215 they had put restraints upon it by forcing John Lackland to accept the Magna Carta which firmly established liberties without example in their day, and which was the basis of the British system. Very different had been the evolution of France. During the Hundred Years War the excesses indulged in by the great feudatories had provoked against them an alliance between Crown and People. The Estates of 1439, by granting Charles VII the right to impose a permanent tax and to maintain an army, virtually abdicated and put their power into his hands. They thus opened for monarchy the way to absolutism; whereas in England the working of her institutions, the greed and turbulence of the Lords, the weakness of a sovereign, opened the way to the worst subversions.

It was at this, for both peoples, historical cross-roads that chance or fate brought upon the scene a princess who was to become the symbol of a dramatic tragedy without precedent.

* Michelet.

Though Margaret of Anjou appears as a character in Shakespeare, not even Shakespeare was able to invoke all the episodes of her fabulous life. A *femme fatale*, an admirable wife, a loving and devoted mother, Chief of State and leader of armies, heroine and executioner; this woman whose beauty was a legend, committed crimes and suffered misfortunes worthy of Greek mythology. Even Marie-Antoinette's story—she, like Margaret, was half Lorraine—cannot bear comparison with it.

The wretched Henry VI's wife never inspired merely reasonable feelings. Her contemporaries seemed forced to choose between adoration and raging hatred. Posterity anathematized her. But posterity never gave her a fair chance, never formed an equitable judgement of the Queen without whom the destinies of France, England and consequently the whole world would have been different.

What is undertaken here is a revision of the arbitrary sentence passed upon her, of her hasty and partisan conviction, for the benefit of the open-minded. After five centuries of loathing, following upon twenty-five years of ordeal, the princess who seemed destined, by her seductiveness, to charm poets, and who yet became the Bloody Rose, figure of the Apocalypse, surely deserves that justice be done to her at last.

# BOOK ONE

# *The Storm*

# *The Europe of 1430*

On 16 July 1429 the army of Charles VII led by Joan of Arc was about to enter Reims.

An atmosphere of marvels and miracle made the lightness of men's hearts the more disturbing. Hardened veterans with scarred and weather-beaten faces, foul-mouthed and blasphemous, their bodies under their armour stinking of hard and bloody labour; butchers of peasants, terror of villagers; warrior-monks vowed to the love of battles, emaciated by the asceticism of war; great noblemen whose brutish vices were combined with fantastic superstitions—all looked, with a fervour bordering on awe, to the peasant girl who was turning their daily life into a manifestation of the supernatural. Recalling the stages of that lightning campaign which was about to transform the 'so-called Dauphin', too poor to afford new shoes, into an authentic King of France, no man doubted that he was serving the direct purpose of the Lord of Hosts and that the fullness of time was upon them.

Only Charles of Valois, between his enthusiastic captains on the one hand and his circumspect councillors on the other, still hesitated to believe in his resurrection.

The King was still the same strange neurotic lad who, morbidly suspicious, would hardly venture upon a bridge and could not stand the sight of a new face. Joan of Arc had brought him the 'sign', for want of which he would have abdicated. Riding towards his exaltation, among the flickering oriflammes, the gleam of armour and weapons and the love of a people turned fanatic, he was perhaps wondering what proof there was that he was not the victim of a prodigious delusion; he may well have wished that he was.

From over the horizon came a small group of horsemen advancing at a canter towards the royal camp. It reined in abruptly, in good order, banner unfurled, and from among his knights René of Anjou, Count of Guise and heir to Bar and Lorraine rode forward to dismount and do homage to his sovereign brother-in-law. There was a clamour of greetings and the King's Captains pressed forward to salute the young prince. At twenty René looked a boy; his face untanned as yet by the winds of campaigning, his sensual mouth set in a brilliant smile, and his naively kind eyes, won him much affection.

His arrival at that particular moment was significant; for, despite his double relationship with Charles VII, the political attitude of his uncle, the Cardinal de Bar, and his father-in-law the Duke of Lorraine connected him with the Anglo-Burgundian party. Quite recently Cardinal Louis had bound himself by a new treaty to the Duke of Bedford, Regent of France for Henry VI. As for Charles the Bold, Duke of Lorraine, he had just refused to provide Joan of Arc with the escort she had asked for to reach the Court. Was this out of pure spite because the Maid, instead of giving him the remedy for his gout which he had asked for, had advised him to quit his mistress, Alison du May, and return to his wife? At all events, the time was not far distant when he would be displaying in derision the King's escutcheon, tied to a horse's tail.

So René of Anjou's presence at the coronation and sacring could be read as a change in the old alliances. Back in the Armagnac fold, the dual Duchy would cover the east flank of the French and serve as a buffer against the Duke of Burgundy. Hence those heartfelt cheers. But did the young prince realize the significance which would be read into his gesture of loyalty? It seems very doubtful.

Carried away by the news of the relief of Orleans and the victory of Patay, as if by the reading of an heroic tale, he had been seized by an irresistible desire to share in the glory won by the royal forces. To the chagrin of his uncle the Cardinal, who had been trimming his sails for ten years to avoid committing himself to any party, he had written to the Duke of Bedford a letter repudiating any possible vassalage to the English Crown. Thereupon, forgetting the danger to the Duchies, and the need which the two old men had of his youth and strength; forgetting even his nineteen-year-old wife, then expecting her third child, he had ridden with all speed to Reims. That was the first time his chivalrous impulsiveness led him to compromise his political interests: it was not to be the last.

The splendid welcome extended to him at Charles' court was not calculated to make him regret his impulse. Riding about reconquered Reims, among a colourful troop of nobles, he relished the delights of the French victory as wholeheartedly as if no parchments lay in his chancery bearing witness to the good understanding and friendly relationships between Lorraine and Burgundy.

In the streets of the ancient city the people shouted for joy. There were many who crossed themselves when the Maid passed, and held out their children towards her. And Merlin's ancient prophecy was recalled: lost for a woman, the kingdom would be saved by a woman. A third woman was to finish Joan's work by destroying the Plantagenets who for three centuries had covered France with their shadow: not that René could have any notion that the child who lay in the womb of his own wife, Isabel of Lorraine, would be that woman.

The Countess Isabel had withdrawn to the château of Pont-à-Mousson for the term of her pregnancy. Despite her youth she felt nothing of the anxiety which would have afflicted most women. Serious, determined and stout-hearted, free from the weaknesses of her sex, of manly sense and courage, she was a true daughter of those eastern marches whose soil nourished the harsher virtues. But in any case the women of that epoch showed none of the timidity and self-effacement which one might have supposed would have been their reaction in an age when the violence of men seemed to reach its atrocious limits.

Less than a century earlier the Countesses of Montfort and of Blois had literally dragged their husbands into the Breton war. In Naples, Queen Joanna, as in Paris, Queen Isabeau, were, in their private lives as in their mode of government, quite as bold as the boldest of men. And very shortly the Countess of Vaudemont would be seen quitting her bed twelve days after her confinement to lead an army to her husband.

Isabel of Lorraine was already showing signs of belonging to that same energetic race of women. Her mother, Margaret of Bavaria, deserted by Duke Charles for that same Alison du May who had born him no fewer than five bastards, had taught her stoicism. By the time she was eighteen Isabel could wear a face unmoved by change of fortune, and accept the disturbing fancies of her charming and frivolous husband.

The news which messengers brought to Pont-à-Mousson might cause the Cardinal, indeed, to groan in secret, but could not fail to raise pride in the young woman's heart. It seemed that René was doing great deeds in the Maid's army: he took part in the seige of Paris; at Chappes he put to flight a strong detachment of Burgundians . . . too brilliant a victory and one for which the imprudent René was to pay dearly later. Meanwhile his own triumph and the flattery with which the French barons were lavish, had gone to his head. He spent the winter at his brother-in-law's side.

Among the echoes of her husband's fame, on 24 March 1430, Isabel of Lorraine gave birth to her second daughter. In René's book of hours, facing the date IX K1. (9 of the Kalends of April), and under the heading *Observations*, the following appears: 'and on the iiith XXIX was born my Lady Margaret, IInd daughter of King René.* The Christian name was apparently chosen in honour of the baby's grandmother, Margaret of Bavaria, who had so meekly and piously born the outrage put upon her by her unworthy husband.

Three months later the sudden death of Cardinal Louis, making René of Anjou Duke of Bar, fetched him hastily home. Six months later again, on 25 January 1431, Charles II, Duke of Lorraine, called the Bold, went to join his one-time enemy and latter-day ally. These two deaths enabled the little princess Margaret to dream her first dreams under a double ducal crown. They also set her, in the tenth month of her age, on a course of trouble and adventures which was to end only with her life.


After 100 years of wars, revolutions, famines and epidemics Europe seemed, in 1430, to reach the ultimate limits of chaos and misery. Since the middle of the fourteenth century the Middle Ages had been in those convulsive throes which heralded their end. Wormeaten and crumbling, their two proud pillars could support them no longer.

Rent and devastated by the Great Schism, the Holy See offered the faithful a spectacle as afflicting as it was

---

* Since the year, at that time, ran from Easter to Easter, the 9th of the Kalends of April 1429 corresponds to 24 March 1430 our style.

ludricous. At one time three Sovereign Pontiffs, supported by three synods were hurling anathemas at each other. Hardly had unity been restored when the Synod of Basle seemed likely to produce yet another anti-Pope.

The Holy Roman Empire which Sigismund himself called 'a ponderous and rusty old machine', was hardly in better case. It was no more than a dilapidated façade, teeming with vermin, a flashy stage-set, against which little men played out their petty ambitions.

As for the Eastern Empire, it was not much more than a single city, Constantinople, which luck and tricks of the basest diplomacy barely preserved from the surrounding barbarians.

Among the nations, England, seemingly the strongest and most unified, was nevertheless half crushed under the burdens of her own victories. Extended from Scotland to the Loire and the Garonne, she had to defend this vast territory with a gravely reduced army and an empty treasury. Bedford had been able to raise hardly 12,000 men to beseige Orleans. On the throne sat an eight-year-old boy surrounded by kinsmen whose mutual hatreds divided the Council and were soon to tear the country itself into factions, aided by a Parliament refusing to grant money. The Cardinal of Winchester had had to pay for his nephew Henry's coronation out of his own pocket and no alms-giving, no liberality of any kind marked this great event. Worthy people growled that even a comfortable burgess could do things better.

And what of France, trodden down by adventurers drawn from half the world and no less cruelly by her friends than by her enemies? That unhappy kingdom seemed to have become a sort of waste-land, a no-man's-land where all men had a free hand to pillage and slaughter. Armagnacs against Burgundians, English against French, even personal rivalries and family feuds were fought out as if the country were a great tilt-yard. The common people paid for the damage; they were lucky even to get a harvest in. Plague raged over a land littered with corpses, and in winter's bitter cold wolves raided Paris and carried off children. In the south, any petty squire was king of a castle and could indulge in the most brutal excesses. In Brittany, Gilles de Rais (Bluebeard) was cutting children's throats by the hundred.

The Spanish kingdoms, suspending their struggle with the Moors, had given themselves over to all the horrors of civil war. Henry III of Castile, finding himself without even the petty cash to pay for his dinner, solved the problem by summoning his principal grandees and forcing them, head on block, to give him what they had.

The Visconti were terrorising Milan. Florence and Pisa were devouring each other. In Naples, Queen Joanna II, at sixty years of age, was still lengthening the list of her lovers, and each new lover meant the adoption of yet another prince, from which whimsical conduct arose endless brawls, and catastrophes without number.

In the north the Hussites were spreading terror from the Vistula to the Rhine. They had ravaged Bohemia and devastated Germany. Year after year their fanatical hordes swept aside the Imperial armies and flowed over the land like burning lava. In their 1430 campaign alone they burned 100 towns and 1,400 villages. Their prisoners were 'impaled, grilled over hot coals, forced to swallow molten lead, torn in four by horses, stoned or drowned'.

An even worse scourge came out of the East: the Turks. They, too, were extending their incursions year after year. Thrace, Greece, Moldavia, Wallachia and Bulgaria had been over-run. 'Wherever the Turks have penetrated,' proclaimed Pope Eugenius IV, 'the country has become barren, the towns have lost their laws and their trades; the Christian religion has neither priests nor altars: humanity has no aid nor refuge left.' And in all Europe there was not one kingdom capable of standing up to these infidels.

Only one Christian prince, the Duke of Burgundy, still had fat provinces, intact and well-governed, and full coffers. His domains were vast and his prestige beyond compare. But even there the edifice was beginning to show cracks in the fabric. His too widely scattered territories were often mutually hostile and it was extremely difficult to impose a single rule on such disparate lands and peoples, so that a thousand contradictions constantly threatened the continued existence of a state so strangely constituted.

Philip of Burgundy exactly summed up, in his person, the second stage feudalism, which had replaced the older feudalism, but which had none of its qualities. Formerly the feudal lord, a native of the lands he ruled, fully symbolised his people who were attached to him by race and tradition. He was, in truth, the head of a family. But since he was nearly always at odds with his immediate noble neighbours, each lord sought his matrimonial and other alliances at a distance; and the laws of succession then coming into play, the most bizarre groupings of heritage resulted. An Angevin reigned in Provence and in Lorraine; an Armagnac at Nemours; a Burgundian in Holland. The lands of any prince who died without direct heirs male gave rise to interminable rivalries. The Hundred Years War had, among its origins, just one such case. In 1430 all Europe was ablaze with a thousand such quarrels, quarrels which were eventually to destroy the feudal system completely.

Well might Tiphaine la Magine, René's old nurse, rocking the baby Margaret of Anjou in her arms, mutter, 'Ah, the poor little thing . . .'* Perhaps the faithful old servant's instinct gave her a premonition of the fate of her charge, of the woman who was to find herself at the

---

* The tomb of this devoted woman can still be seen at Saumur. She is depicted on it holding two little children wearing swaddling clothes in her arms: they are King René and his sister, Marie of Anjou, Queen of France.

conjuncture of so many tragedies—the tragedies of Lorraine, of Naples, of France and England; and who was to contribute more than anyone else to the raising of a new order upon the ruins of the old.

# The Third House of Anjou

The Middle Ages gave to the adjective *Good*, when applied to a prince, a number of meanings all of which were more or less remote from the sense which the word has for us. Thus a *Good* prince was not obliged to be a model of domestic virtue, to be merciful or to have quiet and peaceful tastes. The tyrannical and versatile King John of France was accustomed to indulge in fits of mad rage during which heads were apt to fall. But he had a grand and highly ingenious sense of honour, and was a great man with a battle-axe. He had, moreover, no idea of the value of money, and squeezed his people only to overwhelm his favourites with his generosity. So he was John the Good.

Then there was Philip of Burgundy, the Good Duke: ruthless in pursuit of his ambitions as in pursuit of revenge, greedy, crafty and deplorably immoral, he was nonetheless 'Good' by reason of the facility with which he shed tears, the splendid pomp of his court, and the remarkable number—thirty-seven—of his bastards.

*Good King René*, identity of epithet notwithstanding—in no way resembled either his great grandfather or his cousin. His biographer, Lecoy de Lamarche, is anxious to award his hero all the virtues but is very reluctantly obliged to allow that he was an indifferent soldier and that his heart was too susceptible. Blinded by the devoted affection of his descendants and subjects long after his death, René's virtuous panegyrist even tries to whitewash the latter weakness. But the fact is that nothing in his life served René's reputation as well as his misfortune and his death. For Anjou, as for Provence, he was the last of the Dukes, the last of their Counts; the noble elder, victim of a nephew's cupidity; the unhappy father forced to witness the extinction of his race—hence that atmosphere of tenderness which has kept his memory fresh and fragrant.

In his lifetime public opinion would seem to have been less indulgent. True his patronage of the arts, his talents as a writer, painter of portraits and illuminator of manuscripts, were praised; but praised, as a rule, with a shrug of the shoulders.

The harsh and ferocious fifteenth century did not readily appreciate the meeker virtues in a sovereign and was apt to misconstrue them: René's freedom from cupidity was read as indolence; his readiness to forgive trespasses against him, as cowardice. It was incomprehensible that he should have worked at his portrait of the Duke of Burgundy even in the very prison where the Good Duke was treating him so cruelly. And his detachment from the good things of this world passed the ordinary man's understanding; legends were made of it, and it was said that, hearing that he was to ascend the throne of Naples while engaged in illuminating a manuscript, he did not even pause in his work.

To sum up: Margaret of Anjou's father was a man of rather mediocre intellect and mild spirit, attractive, sensitive, tolerant, incapable of long-term calculation, a fatalist when confronted with an accomplished fact, fond of works of art and craft, of his particular pleasures, and of peace and quiet. He enjoyed jousting, and even serious fighting, but war, for René, was never more than a noble entertainment. And throughout his life he was dominated by a series of women.

In 1430 the woman who ruled him was his mother, Yolande of Aragon, Queen of the Two Sicilies, Duchess of Anjou, the least known and most misunderstood princess in all history, though her features and legend were to become as familiar to Frenchmen as those of Henry of Navarre or Richelieu.

Introduced against her will and despite solemn protests into the house of the hereditary enemies of her family and her race, this energetic Spaniard became their most vigorous champion. She managed their stormy affairs with a skill, a suppleness and a total want of scruple which makes her the equal of the greatest chiefs of state.

The third House of Anjou inherited from its two predecessors an almost frantic ambitiousness. The first of these, the Plantagents, rulers of England and two thirds of France, had reached its zenith with Henry V whose son, the boy king Henry VI, wore the crowns both of William the Conqueror and Saint Louis. The second House of Anjou, issue of Charles, third son of Louis VIII, had reigned over Sicily, Naples, Provence, Hungary, Poland, Moldavia and Wallachia, and the Dalmatian provinces.

By giving the title of Duke of Anjou to Louis, his second son, scion of the third dynasty, King John the Good seemed to have opened to him prospects which were limitless. And from his youth this prince astonished his contemporaries by his unquenchable thirst for titles and domains. Not satisfied with Anjou, raised to the dignity of a peerage, with the County* of Maine, and the government of Languedoc, he kept a close check on all fiefs about to change hands, so that he could seize the first opportunity to swoop on them with the single-minded promptitude of a stooping hawk. His lands and castles became countless but he wanted more, he wanted a royal crown.

Soon disinherited sovereigns or their needy heirs got to

* As we should say, earldom.

know where they could find a profitable market for old, questionable claims. Isabel of Montferrat, daughter of King James of Majorca, dispossessed by an Aragonese prince, sold Louis her paper rights; so, too, did James of Baux who claimed to be heir to the Eastern Empire through his ancestors the Courtenays. Whereafter Louis called himself Emperor of Constantinople, King of Jerusalem, King of Majorca and Cyprus, Prince of Achaea and the Morea, Duke of Clarence, Count of Rousillon—all of which titles were as grandiloquent as they were, alas, void of substance.

He thought he had hold of something better when the head of the second house of Anjou, Joanna I, Queen of the Two Sicilies, the romantic Queen who was so popular by reason of her crimes, her misfortunes and her love affairs, first adopted him and then made him her heir. Louis was Regent of France at the time, his brother Charles V having just died. By looting the whole country and thereby sowing the seeds of future revolts, he managed to get together the money required to lead an army into Italy. But he never even reached the point of actually fighting Charles of Duras, in whose veins ran the blood of the Neapolitan Angevins, for his kingdom. His army melted away in a few months and he himself died of the plague at Bari. At least, however, he had annexed Provence.

His son Louis II was no more successful than him in planting his standard on the towers of the Castle of the Egg. Unlucky in Italy, in France he was powerful in the royal councils in which he espoused the Armagnac interest. His wife, Yolande of Aragon, was already forcing her own opinions on him. It was she who, at the castle of Marcoussis in October 1413 at a meeting decisive for France's future, arranged with Isabeau of Bavaria that Charles, Count of Ponthieu, the youngest son of Charles VI, should marry Marie of Anjou, daughter of the King of the Two

43

Sicilies. The combined ages of the betrothed couple totalled nineteen.

As soon as the betrothal ceremony was concluded, Yolande took her future son-in-law to Angers. This was to have considerable consequences: for had Yolande not constituted herself the boy's foster-mother, had she not removed the future Charles VII from Isabeau's appalling Court, not even Joan of Arc could have saved France's soul.

Circumstances were soon to make Yolande the pivot of the 'national' party. The death of Duke Louis II in 1417 left her with the task of defending the Duchy of Anjou for her three sons, all of them minors. In the same year her son-in-law became Dauphin, white hope of all loyal Frenchmen. But had it not been for that watchful guardian of his, what sort of hope could he have been or had, repudiated as he was by his own mother? The Treaty of Troyes stripped him of his heritage, his kingdom had no capital, no treasury and only the remnant of an army. Confronted by Henry VI of England and France, his triumphant rival, he had only a single support, a single refuge, a single source of council: the House of Anjou; Yolande.

She showed her admirable mettle during the years of trial—1420 to 1429. She enjoyed the exercise of power without seeking its appearance, if only because she knew that her actions were more effective if they did not seem to be her own. Passionately determined that her family should be great; subtle, tenacious, realistic and generous; she laid her plans with cool precision and executed them unwaveringly. She was not scrupulous as to means. Even though the claim that she procured Agnes Sorel for her son-in-law is absurd because of the dates in question, there is no reason to think that she drew the line at that kind of thing. For, indifferent to love on her own account, she was clever at exploiting the sexual weaknesses of her associates, preferred suggestion and persuasion to force, and would always sacrifice her property to her policy. She was to die a ruined woman, having, as she says in her last will and testament, dedicated her wealth to the cause of the Kings of France and Sicily. It was a mighty task that Yolande, in her discreet widow's weeds, accomplished without ostentation.

It was she who twice—in 1421 and 1424—saved Anjou from the English. It was she who recruited a Scottish army for France, reconciled the king and the Bretons, and caused Richemont to be appointed Constable of France. A determined enemy of Charles VII's favourites, she broke several of them but was checkmated by the last, Georges de la Trémoille, who would have been quite satisfied with a France reduced to Languedoc, Dauphiné and a few southern towns. And since it was at this moment that the English launched their supreme offensive and laid siege to Orleans, there remained only the oft-heralded miracle to hope for.

It was then that the Maid appeared in Vaucouleurs and applied to Robert de Baudricourt, *a vassal of René of Anjou*; and that Baudricourt, having turned her away once, gave her the means of getting to Charles's Court.

Joan, as we know, reached it despite an ambush laid by La Trémoille who was convinced that she was an agent of his old enemy, Yolande. At all events, it was the Count of Vendôme, Yolande's ally, who stood Joan's sponsor at Chinon, and it was Yolande who stood guarantor for the girl's honour. What is not so well known is that it was among her Angevins and her Manceaus, and among the Bretons of her friend Richemont, who was in disgrace at the time, that the old queen raised the army with which the Maid faced Orleans and opened the way to Reims.

Meanwhile Yolande of Aragon was wisely governing her son Duke Louis III's provinces, and setting him in his father's and grandfather's footsteps on the road to Naples. And she succeeded in getting his younger brother René adopted by his uncle, the Cardinal of Bar, and in betrothing him to Isabel, heiress to Lorraine.

This latter success was considered a masterpiece of diplomacy. Was it, Europe's princes and statesmen wondered, intended to contrive a back door into Burgundian territory for the English? Or would it, on the other hand, bring all the Eastern Marches back under French influence? Everyone was waiting with bated breath for the repercussions of Duke Charles's death; but nobody foresaw the consequences of the war which was to result from it.

Furious at seeing the Duchy fall to his cousin Isabel, Antoine of Vaudémont, Charles the Bold's nephew, scarcely waited for his uncle's death to protest against what he considered his spoliation. Thanks to René's illconsidered exploits on behalf of Charles VII, he was able to count on Duke Philip of Burgundy's support. With that alliance assured, he proclaimed himself the only rightful heir to Lorraine, that territory being a masculine fief. He raised his standard against the new prince, called on Burgundy for help, and received a small force commanded by Marshal de Tourlongeon. René of Anjou called his vassals to his colours, and appealed to France.

But the reins of government were still in La Trémoille's hands. Was the House of Anjou's desertion of Joan of Arc* a result of this situation? At all events, there was a reconciliation between Yolande and the King's favourite; the Maid had to march almost alone to the relief of besieged Compiègne, and René was given a small French army commanded by Barbazan, a veteran and distinguished soldier.

The war began.

* Joan was made a prisoner at Compiègne as a result of La Trémoille's manoeuvres and those of his associate, Archbishop Regnault of Chartres.

Isabel of Lorraine had been stoical when her husband had gone off to the wars in search of fame and fortune. But already in the first year of her life the baby Margaret must have been aware of all the anxieties of a mother who saw her happiness, her crown, and her child's whole future at the mercy of the fortunes of war.

On 2 July 1431, the two adversaries clashed at Bulgnéville. René had more men, but Tourlongeon had taken up an excellent position. Wisely, Barbazan advised that an engagement should be avoided and that René should confine the action to one of attrition. This cautious temporising did not suit the dashing Lorrainers, many of them at their first battle and on fire to win their spurs. They accused Barbazan of cowardice; the old warrior forgot his prudence, and crying that putting the matter to test would soon show who among them had the stoutest heart, gave battle.

In a few hours, and despite their courage, the French and the Lorrainers, ill-disciplined as they were and put at a disadvantage by the enemy's superior position, began to give ground before the Burgundians. Fighting desperately, Barbazan, in the forefront of the battle, was killed, and from that moment defeat turned into a rout. As usual many of the vanquished performed deeds of prowess which might win the heart of a mistress but were otherwise quite useless. René could perfectly well have disengaged his forces and withdrawn, or got away himself, thus minimizing the consequence of his failure; and all the more easily in that the people of the countryside were for the most part loyal to him. He chose instead to play the *preux chevalier*, was taken prisoner, and thus changed a temporary setback into an irredeemable disaster for which he had to pay for the rest of his life.

Delighted at the idea of having so magnificent a prey in his clutches, Philip of Burgundy hastened to get his cousin into his own hands. He shut him up at first in his castle of Talent, then had him moved to the donjon of Bacon-sur-Salins in Franche-Comté, being determined to extract every ounce of advantage from this marvellous stroke of luck.

Deprived of both their prince and their army, it seemed as if the Duchies of Lorraine and Bar must collapse into anarchy. But the Duchess Isabel, now twenty-two years of age, had the heart and soul of a hero. Within a few weeks a Council of Regency had been constituted, Antoine of Vaudémont thrown back, and a truce concluded with the Duke of Burgundy. For Philip the Good, now that he held the ace of trumps, was quite willing to prolong the game. Secretly encouraged by him, John of Luxembourg, one of the Duke's vassals, took advantage of the situation to seize the county of Guise, an apanage of René's to which he maintained that he had a legitimate claim. Isabel protested in vain.

René asked the Burgundian to allow him temporary freedom on parole, in order to restore order in his states. The Good Duke agreed to do so; but on what conditions! René was to hand over both his sons as hostages as well as four of his castles. Philip was to be sole arbiter in the matter of the succession to Lorraine. And René was to come to terms with John of Luxemburg touching the cession of the county of Guise. In exchange, Philip granted René his freedom for a term of one year: 1 May 1432 to 1 May 1433.

The young captive prince agreed to everything. On his way home he stopped at the castle of Bohain to see John of Luxembourg, the rascally 'gentleman' who had grabbed the Maid at Compiègne and sold her for 10,000 pounds. René responded with good grace to his host's courtesies; he never learned the art of bearing a grudge against his enemies. The county of Guise was ceded to John, who paid its former proprietor an indemnity of 20,000 pounds.

At that epoch every important contract was ratified by a marriage. René promised his two-year-old daughter Margaret to the Count of Saint-Pol, John of Luxembourg's brother, and the two men parted on the best of terms. Moreover, shortly thereafter another compromise did something to patch up the Anjou-Vaudémont quarrel for the time being: the two parties undertook to submit their case to arbitration by the Duke of Burgundy. Meanwhile, Ferry de Vaudémont, Antoine's son, was betrothed to Yolande of Anjou, Margaret's elder sister.

According to a romantic legend these two young people are supposed to have been passionately in love with each other: the princess, fearing that her father might change his mind, is said to have eloped with the handsome Ferry. There is, alas, only one thing wrong with this pretty tale: in 1433 Yolande was scarcely four years old. True, she was handed over to the Vaudémont family, but solely in order to respect an old custom: children betrothed by their parents while they were still in the cradle were brought up together. Only chance, or perhaps a parental afterthought, prevented Margaret from growing to girlhood at the third-rate court of Bohain Castle.

An unexpected stroke of luck now gave René a chance to wipe out the consequences of his setbacks. Philip of Burgundy, beginning to wish for a reconciliation with France, decided to use his paroled prisoner as official Ambassador to Charles VII and Yolande of Aragon. René readily fell in with this proposal, if only because it saved him from having to return to his fortress-prison on the agreed date. If he succeeded in his mission, he might hope to come well out of the business himself. A blunder ruined his chances.

Despite his promise that Philip should be sole arbiter, he had submitted the question of Lorraine to the suzerain of the Duchy, the Emperor Sigismund. As it happened Sigismund and Philip the Good were on bad terms:

irritated by an act of bad faith on Philip's part, Sigismund unexpectedly brought up the Lorraine affair, and found in favour of the House of Anjou. Philip, beside himself with rage, not only demanded that René surrender to his parole immediately, but treated his prisoner with a harshness quite contrary to knightly custom.

Transferred to the dismal castle of Dijon, the captive now had to live the unhappiest days of his life. The elegant prince whose garments had been scented with musk, the dashing cavalier who had been the idol of every court beauty, was transformed into a poor, neglected wretch with an untrimmed beard. All contact with the outside world was forbidden him. The coarsest food took the place of those refined banquets which he had taken pleasure in arranging. Only his poetry and his painting brought him a measure of relief in his misery. And this was the moment chosen by an ironical or malign fate to overwhelm him with what, in other circumstances, would have been the greatest and least-expected good fortune.

On 12 November 1434, the death of his elder brother Louis III gave René Anjou, Maine and Provence, all real and substantial legacies, as well as a number of high-sounding titles to other empty honours. And on 2 January 1435 Joanna II of Duras, last heiress to the second House of Anjou (so long at mortal enmity with the third), died leaving him the kingdom of the Two Sicilies which her people had been unable to conquer for her.

The aged Queen, whose whimsical lusts were to help plunge Europe into a century of war, had first adopted Alphonso V of Aragon, then Louis III of Anjou, her own rival. Louis dead, she had chosen René, who thus inherited all the claims and rights of the two rival families.

A radiant and diverse empire! Lorraine, severe and hardworking; the opulent serenity of the Angevin countryside starred with sumptuous castles and manors; the gold and azure of Provence; Naples with its gorgeous

associations; and the almost legendary Sicily. To say nothing of the Oriental and Spanish cloud-cuckoo-land. The
bay of Naples, the Meuse, the Loire and the Rhône to be
governed by a single sceptre! It was typical of the absurd
if charming combinations produced by the play of the
new feudal system. Chance, by endowing them with
estates which, as it were, cancelled each other out, inflicted
the tortures of Tantalus on Europe's princes. They found
themselves engaged in a perpetual race from one to another,
obliged to watch the North slip between their fingers the
moment they had recovered a firm grasp on the South.

Nevertheless, what a prospect, what a dream for a poor
devil whose actual horizon was limited to a sentry's pike
and the iron bars of a cell window; on the other hand, what
a torment to know that so great a treasure was slipping out
of his grasp because he was not there to take charge of it.

Already master of Sicily, Alphonso of Aragon was now
laying claim to Naples. Fortunately, his fleet was caught by
the combined Milanese and Genoese fleets—both cities
were allies of the Angevin party—and cut to pieces off
Gaeta. And he himself fell into the enemy's hands. For
René this was the decisive moment, his great chance; but
to seize it, he had to be free, and the Good Duke Philip
obstinately refused to suggest any terms, any kind of
accommodation. Before agreeing to the Treaty of Arras he
even went so far as to require that the matter of his cousin
should not be raised. René gave way to despair, resigned to
wasting his youth in a prison cell, while his French
dominions fell into confusion and his fine Italian crown to
the Aragonese.

Isabel of Lorraine did not see the matter in that light at
all. A worthy daughter of a line which for centuries aimed
at every throne in Europe (and was to continue doing so in
the Guise and Habsburg-Lorraine branches), she rejoiced
in the realisation that she could now gratify her tastes for
adventure simply by doing her duty as a loyal wife. Leaving

her States in the charge of a new Council of Regency, she went to Dijon and obtained from her husband full powers as his Lieutenant-General. Whereafter, having placed her children in a safe refuge, and turned her plate, jewels and everything of value she possessed into money, this twenty-four-year old wife of a helpless captive set out from Nancy to Naples bent on the conquest of a kingdom.

Some historians, and those not the least considerable, have held that Margaret accompanied her mother in the course of this adventure, an escapade which Ariosto might have imagined. It is no longer possible to entertain that version of the story. Irrefutable documents prove that René's daughter was in Anjou during the years in question. Margaret was left in the charge of her grandmother, the illustrious Queen Yolande, and received her education in Angers castle, far from the tumult in the kingdom of Naples.

Luck, as if captivated by her boldness, at first smiled on Isabel. Having survived a number of spectacular dangers, the Queen succeeded in reaching Naples, and in setting up a government in her husband's name. Then, however, the tide of her enemies began to rise, its waves beat at the walls of the Castle of the Egg and the *Castel Nuovo*, and Alphonso of Aragon entered them as victor. The Angevins put up a heroic fight but their efforts were paralysed by their leader's absence. Philip the Good was approached again and the Duke at last deigned to formulate proposals which were firm, albeit preposterous. Margaret of Anjou must marry the Count of Charolais, heir to the Duchy of Burgundy. Her dowry, payable immediately, must include Bar-le-Duc, Pont-à-Mousson, Cassel and a number of other, less important, territories. Finally René must undertake to pay a ransom of 1,000,000 gold *livres*.

The Duke's exhorbitant demands caused René's nego-tiators to withdraw in consternation. Months of new approaches and obstinate haggling were required before a more or less viable treaty was drawn up. But at last, on 8 November 1436, the drawbridge of Dijon castle was lowered for a man carried away by the excitement of realizing that he was free, young, and a King, once more to experience the intoxication of wild, headlong gallops, of lances broken in a splendour of plumes and banners, of bewitching smiles from beauties who could refuse no favour to a prince still only thirty years old. René forgot the price of those delights—abandonment of his claims on Nieppe, Cassel and Dunkerque; homage to be paid for Pont-à-Mousson, and an undertaking to pay 400,000 gold crowns. For seventeen months he even forgot his wife and those champions of his cause and crown who were awaiting him as a Messiah.

Not until 12 April 1438 did he set out for Naples. Installed, after many adventures, in his capital, for four years he enjoyed a reign of feasts, combats, gallantries and heroic-dramatic adventures. But Alphonso of Aragon's craft and obstinacy at last got the upper hand. Despite a memorable defence, Naples fell to the Spaniards on 2 June 1442, and René and Isabel joined the company of kings without kingdoms They made their way to their French estates where they found themselves, exhausted, penniless and yet still dazzled, as if only just awakening from some fantastic dream.

While her parents were thus experiencing the fickleness of fortune, Margaret of Anjou was growing in beauty and learning. Trained by excellent masters, her mind assimilated everything in the way of knowledge which her epoch was capable of teaching a girl. Her brother's preceptor was Antoine de la Salle, the clever and perspicacious author of *Le Petit Jehan de Saintré*; there can be no doubt that he took pleasure in completing the education of so remarkable a child.

From all her ancestors she had inherited contempt for physical fatigue, a love of hunting, horses and warlike spectacles; from her father, keen artistic sensibility, that taste for refinements which the austere northern peoples held blameworthy in the southerners; from her mother, tenacity, courage and contempt for obstacles. The distaff and her book of hours were destined to play only a secondary rôle in her life.

Yolande of Aragon, having finally ensured the kingdom's future after La Trémoille's fall in 1433, had six years later entrusted the country's direction to hands she could rely on. Thereafter she herself concentrated on the administration of the House of Anjou's French provinces and the education of her grandchildren. The wise Queen seems to have made up her mind to familiarize the young princess with public business as early as possible. Thus, as early as the years 1440 to 1443, on several occasions we find Margaret ratifying and certifying various payments or settlements of accounts.

Writers who were Margaret's contemporaries, whether dramatists or historians, have left us a wide range of opposed opinions of her character, her morals and her policies; on one thing they were all agreed—her beauty. From the age of thirteen the young princess charmed the eye of all beholders; the mere sight of her portrait was apt to arouse transports of love. But apart from some more or less lyrical descriptions, there are few documents enabling us to give an exact picture of such remarkable graces. The few representations we have of her show a haughty carriage of the head, a mouth which is disdainful, although the lips reveal sensuality, and very fine eyes which it must have been hard to make her lower.

Many nobles aspired to her hand. After the Counts of Saint-Pol and Charolais, came the Count of Nevers, the Duke of Burgundy's nephew; for a brief while he enjoyed the honour of being admitted as her betrothed, but was soon displaced by a more illustrious rival: Frederick of Habsburg, recently elected Emperor, was seeking a wife fit to share with him the crown of Charlemagne. The chroniclers were singing of the King of Sicily's daughter as a marvel; he wanted her, and sent an impressive embassy into France to ask for her hand. This was that Frederick III who, while discrediting his name by his manifold baseness, yet founded the fortunes of his family by an astonishingly successful policy of marriages, (*Tu, Felix Austria, Nube*); and died, after a reign of half a century, of a surfeit of melons.

His ambassadors were received at Saumur by Yolande with much pomp and circumstance. All the splendour which the bankrupt court could still conjure up, was deployed in their honour. Margaret was dazzling. And as it happens we know, thanks to King René, the exact sums which were spent on making the most of her beauty. Master Guillaume de la Planche, Merchant of Angers, furnished 'eleven ells of cloth of gold, violet, crimson and *forse* at thirty crowns the ell and 1,000 small pieces of vair.'* In addition, one Master Castaignier, furrier provided 'ten dozen *letices*' for white fur to edge the dress. We even know that a charge of fifteen francs, seven sous and six deniers, was made for the canvas, paper and cord for packing, and for transport from Angers to Saumur.

King René of Sicily being absent, nothing was concluded. Nevertheless, the Ambassadors departed laden with presents and good words. Yolande believed her grand-daughter's future magnificently provided for, and, feeling her work accomplished, allowed herself the indulgence of dying at Saumur, in the hôtel of the Lord of Tucé where she had been living, on 14 November 1442.

---

* A fur obtained from a variety of squirrel with grey back and white belly, much used in the thirteenth and fourteenth centuries as a trimming for garments. An ell was forty-five inches.

But Margaret was not to seize this chance of escaping her fate. She was not destined peacefully to procreate the family which was to have dominion in the future; but to bring down, in an ocean of blood, the blood of a million men, one of the proudest fabrics of Europe's past.

# Peace by Love

13 March 1444—the Earl of Suffolk has disembarked at Harfleur . . .

From Normandy, still under English rule, across the desert of the Ile-de-France, through a Paris still lying fallow and an Orléanais still trembling to the march and counter-march of armed men, to the oasis of the Loire, the news passed from town to town, rekindling everywhere small fires of hope which had seemed for ever extinguished.

Flickering, smoky and at the mercy of every breath of wind, the tiny flame of peace was barely kindled, yet shone like a sun. No man dared look steadily at it. The idea that there might now be an end to the killings, rapings, sacking of towns, all the violence which for thirty years had transformed the kingdom into a hell of beggars, rogues and vagabonds, seemed a mirage fitted only to deceive and turn men's heads. And yet . . .

. . . Yet William de la Pole, Earl of Suffolk, Ambassador Extraordinary from England's King had certainly set foot in France, his mission to lay the foundations of an accord which would relegate a century of war to the province of history.

His mandate was a crushing burden, his task a prodigious one. The dangers implicit in success were hardly less than those implicit in failure: even before setting out

Suffolk had asked and obtained, in advance, absolution for 'any errors of judgement into which he might fall.'

His mission was a consequence of internecine strife, even more bitter and harsh than open warfare. Neither Joan of Arc's intervention, nor Burgundy's defection, nor the loss of Paris, nor failures at Lagny, la Charité and Pontoise, nor even a last and shameful defeat outside Dieppe had sufficed to reduce English pride to the point of contemplating peace. Still more had been required—old fratricidal hates revived, the revolt of the bishops moved by avarice, and half a palace revolution.

From the moment when the jealous gods had removed Henry V at the zenith of his triumph, England had been given over to warring passions between members of her Royal family. The nine-months-old King left to her by the victor of Agincourt clearly could not act as mediator.

The Queen, Catherine of Valois, had set the bad example. Her husband was hardly cold in his grave before she, whose patriotic senses had refused to be aroused by the conquering Englishman's embraces, threw herself into the arms of a Welshman, scarcely more than a mere country gentleman, Owen Tudor. Greatly scandalizing her subjects, she had born him two children. Stripped of her rights and privileges and relegated to Bermondsey Abbey, this daughter of Charles VI, who had brought her husband the French crown by way of dowry, there perished of misery at the age of thirty-six.

Among the English princes one only, the Duke of Bedford, Regent of France, Henry V's brother and the eldest of the family, was endowed with political talent. He died early, leaving Luck free to transfer her favours to Charles VII.

His brother, Humphrey of Gloucester, Lord Protector of England, filled London with the spectacle of his extravagances. For ever brawling, drinking, outraging any woman who took his fancy, spending money like water, his vices won him the adulation of the mob and the hatred of the Church party, all-powerful because most of the public wealth was in its hands.

In the Council the Bishops were dominant. Their leader was the famous Beaufort, Cardinal of Winchester, initiator of the trial of Joan of Arc. This prelate was consumed by the demon of ambition and a touchy, quick-tempered pride. The son of John of Gaunt, Duke of Lancaster and Catherine Swynford, and uncle of Henry V and his brothers, he nourished a blind, almost maniacal hatred of Gloucester. Brawls between the servants of the lord temporal and the lord spiritual daily let blood in the London streets.

The Lord Protector's folly was his fall: by daring to marry Jacqueline of Hainaut, Countess of Holland, who was in revolt against her suzerain, Philip of Burgundy, he alienated his least dispensable ally and so gave his enemy the advantage. Firmly seated on his sacks of gold, Winchester seized the reins of government. But the conquest of France was still draining the country's blood and treasure.

The clergy were appalled at the cost of this war, for it was they who carried the financial burden. It was impoverishing even the nobles. For a long time the only pay received by the English military leaders had been French lands. They, knowing their tenure precarious, wrung the last penny of profit out of them by every kind of extortion. But although their manors might be bursting with loot, they were forced to pawn it to feed their followers. As for the common people of England, such was their condition that not even the French could envy them.

So peace began to be whispered about like an impious word. English necks had been so stiffened by Crécy, Poitiers and Agincourt that they could not bend to admit defeat at last.

Gloucester was the personification of that bellicose intransigence. Naturally, Winchester and his party took the opposing view. But they dared not openly say the monstrous thing which was in their minds: that England must recognize the fact that she had, during the past fifteen years, ceased to be invincible and that her conquests were crumbling away. To give them the courage to do so, they needed a war hero on their side.

The Earl of Suffolk had filled the two kingdoms with the tale of his prowess. He had been commander-in-chief at Orleans when Joan saved the city. The French, having taken him at Jargaux, had shown at what price they valued his abilities by setting his ransom at the fabulous figure of 2,400,000 *livres*. But his fame no longer sufficed if it did not bring him power. Confronted by, on the one hand, a Gloucester still young and full of passions, on the other, Cardinal Beaufort who was greedy and despotic but nearly eighty years old, Suffolk's ambition showed him at once where a succession to power might be hoped for. So this warrior breathed life into the peace party.

It would be unjust to attribute to him purely personal motives for his conduct. Clear-sighted, the Earl judged that England ran the risk of losing the fruit of her victories entirely, if she did not make the best of things as they were. Only the making of a number of relatively minor concessions could now save the really important parts of England's conquests—Guyenne, Normandy and Calais. But before he could act, Gloucester must be neutralised, and the Protector's popularity made him dangerous. He had one weak point—his wife; he must be attacked at that point.

The Duke had compromised England's chances for the love of Jacqueline of Hainaut; then forgot her as soon as he set eyes on one of her ladies, Eleanor Cobham; baseborn and an adventuress though she was, her Olympian beauty hiding a pernicious spirit, he married her, calmly defying the anathemas which the Church holds over bigamists.

The splendour of her rise and the honours and glory of

being the first lady in the land were not enough to content the insatiable Eleanor. She wanted a crown, wanted it with that morbid intensity with which lesser courtesans may desire some particular gem. And there was so little between her and her heart's desire—a sick and inexperienced boy. But that boy might marry, beget children; and in that case the Duchess would never make the royal entry into the city, the vision of which had become an obsesssion. She must take a hand herself.

Soon she was surrounding herself with necromancers and witches. Having consulted the spirits, she involved herself in still more evil practices. Amidst a *décor* which can only be called demonic, wax figurines of Henry VI were nightly melted, or stuck with needles through the heart. Since, according to the belief of the times, these operations could not fail to produce the victim's death, to make use of them was tantamount to murder.

Winchester's spies got wind of these goings on. One of Eleanor's servants was arrested and confessed. The Duchess was arrested. The shock was tremendous: an accusation of treason and witchcraft was the one charge against which 'the good Duke Humphrey's' power and popularity were helpless. Among the accused were '. . . master Thomas Southwell, a canon of St Stephen's chapel at Westminster, master John Hun, a chaplain of the said Duchess, and master Roger Bolingbrooke, a cunning necromancer, and a woman called Margery Jordeine, surnamed the Witch of Eye beside Winchester, to whose charge it was laid that they, at the request of the said Duchess, had devised an image of wax representing the King, which by their sorcery by little and little consumed, intending thereby in conclusion to waste and destroy the King's person.'[*] Eleanor's accomplices were burnt at the stake; the Duchess herself was condemned to three days public penance, dressed only in a shift and being dragged

[*] Holinshead, vol. 3, p. 204.

round London in a cart. Torch in hand, she underwent this dreadful calvary and thereafter she was incarcerated in Chester, Kenilworth, and finally the Isle of Man.

The Cardinal and Suffolk waited, hoping perhaps that Gloucester would rebel. To the general amazement, he made no move. He seemed to be beaten. The peace party could declare itself.

The first thing to be done was to get the King married. Even Gloucester had been thinking on those lines and had been negotiating a marriage between Henry VI and the Count of Armagnac's daughter. That great nobleman, insolently rich and in open rebellion against Charles VII, was tyrannizing all the south of France from the rocky heights where his castle was poised. The Protector had thought that he would find in Armagnac an ally able and willing to cover Guyenne; and a royal father-in-law rich enough to refill the Treasury. But Winchester would not hear of a princess who was not to owe her crown to himself: it was easy to foresee the power which any tolerably clever woman would have over the king.

Henry VI at twenty-one was a child, gentle and timid and given over to his studies and religious devotions. He had had nothing to do with any woman since his mother had been taken from him. He made a cult of Catherine's memory and bore an obstinate grudge against Gloucester, the author of her misfortunes. It seemed a simple matter to persuade him to fall in love.

But with whom? For a brief while the Cardinal thought of one of Charles VII's eight daughters. But the past was not to be so easily and deeply buried; better to choose a bride who was not so grand a lady; such a one, moreover, would be under a great obligation to the engineers of her good fortune.

The story of Margaret of Anjou's charms had long since crossed the Channel. Champchevrier, a French knight, a prisoner on parole in London, never wearied of vaunting them. As the daughter of a king, but without a kingdom, nearly ruined, closely connected with Charles VII, and just made to arouse a young man's love, the princess Margaret seemed made to meet the case. The King was told about her, his interest was caught, he expressed a wish to see at least a portrait of his enchanting cousin. Champchevrier was entrusted with the mission of fetching one from France.

Since Gloucester was by no means willing to indulge his nephew in this whim, the embassy was shrouded in noveletish mystery. Champchevrier, however, returned safe and sound to Westminster, bearing the priceless miniature which was to have a devastating effect on the political life of the Continent. When Henry saw it, the springs of his youth seemed to be released at last. The picture was to him so much captive sunshine; it seemed to have all the radiance of the smiling South, that bold, smooth, vital brilliance, which is only to be met with under cloudless skies. Margaret bore clearly in her face the imprint of her Spanish blood.

The King's decision was quickly taken: this girl, and none other, must share his throne. And with that sovereign sanction to support them, the bishops of the Council made their first overtures to Charles VII, who received them with benevolent courtesy.

Such, however, were the dangers to be foreseen, that nobody dared go directly to the essence of the business. No question of doing more than negotiate the conditions of the marriage and of a truce during which the matters at issue would be studied, solutions to problems sought . . .

For already the mere notion of reconciliation between the century-long enemies was making the real intransigents foam at the mouth. Gloucester's friends raised a terrible outcry. And there were many people who, wishful though they might be to see the advent of less troubled times, did not dare publicly to bear the stigma of so cowardly an opinion. There were even many Frenchmen who showed their ill humour at the turn of events: captains of armed bands worried about their livelihood; usurers who had lent money to the Crown and who might now have to curb their tyrannical rapacity; and veteran warriors greedy for the chance to win an outright victory.

By prudence and energy, Charles VII and Winchester overcame all the obstacles.

The Count of Armagnac breathed fire and slaughter. The Dauphin Louis—subsequently Louis XI—by way of opening his campaign against the feudatories, set out for the south and having, by the simple device of perjuring himself, taken the famous castle, put the Count out of the way of doing any more mischief. In England, the bishops silenced the opposition; Suffolk wrung plenary powers from Parliament, not to mention absolution in advance; and sailed for France.

The French court learned of his arrival on 31 March 1444.

Charles VII, driven out of Paris by the ravages of plague, famine and bands of ruffians, was at Tours. Hastily, he summoned his Council and it was decided to welcome the English Ambassador in style. The King of Sicily and his brother Charles of Anjou were delegated to ride out and meet him.

Ever since the collapse of his Neapolitan dream, René had given himself up completely to playing his part as a peer of France, with credit. A rather superficial study of public business, the administration of his estates, poetry, drawing, planning his future castles, and occasionally a noble *fête* which emptied his pockets for some time to come, such were the matters which filled his days. As attractive as ever, René was very much in his brother-in-law's good books; his credit in that quarter was based on several, but all equally firm, foundations: the charm of his character; a loyalty which could not be eroded by fac-

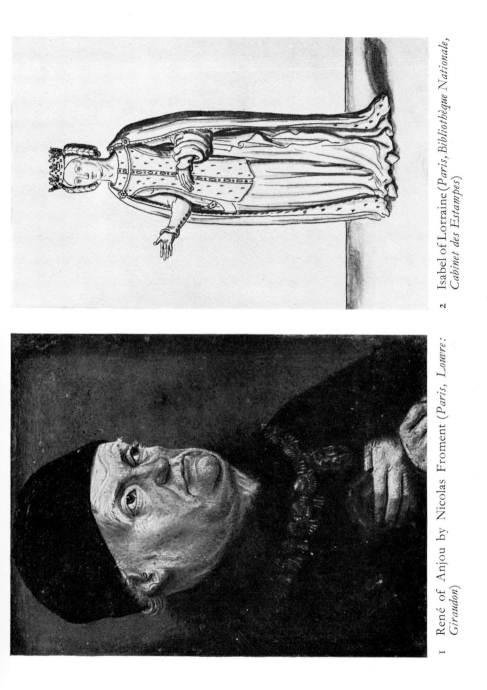

1 René of Anjou by Nicolas Froment (*Paris, Louvre: Giraudon*)

2 Isabel of Lorraine (*Paris, Bibliothèque Nationale, Cabinet des Estampes*)

3   Effigy of Charles VI, Abbey of St-Denis, near Paris (*Wim Swaan*)

4   Effigy of Isabeau of Bavaria, queen of Charles VI, Abbey of St-Denis, near Paris (*Wim Swaan*)

titious temptations; the shared memory of Yolande. But there was still something else.

When, at the beginning of the year 1443, Isabel of Lorraine made her first appearance at the Court which her almost manly heroism had kept her from until that moment, she was accompanied by half a dozen maids of honour, all that remained of her ephemeral royalty. One of these ladies shone, among her colleagues, with a brilliance which was not long in fascinating Charles himself. Within a few months, Agnes Sorel became the *Dame de Beauté*, the King's inspiration, his 'official mistress', first of her kind in France. She never failed in gratitude to her first protectors; the course of these negotiations which were to be of such material advantage to the Angevins owed a good deal to her influence.

On 16 April 1444, René and his brother met Suffolk with grand ceremony. On the following day they escorted him to the chateau of Montils, which was the King's residence for the time being; and the negotiations, which were to be decisive, began.

The Ambassador asked, officially, for Madame Margaret's hand. The Kings of France and Sicily readily agreed to the proposed alliance. But they did not want to deceive their cousin of England: the princess was poor, not only had Italy absorbed René's fortune, but his future revenues were mortgaged by his debt to the Duke of Burgundy to whom he still owed the greater part of his ransom.

No matter: The lady's birth and personal graces would be sufficient dowry even for a queen-to-be. And as for her trousseau, the whole nation of England would feel it an honour to provide it. Well, but, insinuated King Charles the parsimonious, the expenses of travelling from the Loire to the Thames were very considerable and in the present state of French finances . . . Well, then, Henry VI would pay the bill out of the privy purse.

Which details being settled, the King could come to the really important business and did so without beating about the bush: on the very eve of peace, could the English king still hold on to his father-in-law's property, Anjou and Maine to wit? As for Anjou, a mere verbal renunciation would suffice; the invader had never effectively laid hands on that province formerly intended for the Duke of Bedford. But Maine was another matter—the gateway to Normandy, whose conquest had been costly in blood and treasure; where for twenty years many English lords had made their home. . . .

It was Suffolk, then, who beat about the bush; he seemed to hear howls of rage even from the least of London's citizens as they saw their prey snatched from them. Charles played the high-handed victor: Maine or nothing. Suffolk realised that he was about to give his enemies a terrible weapon to attack him with, that he was condemning himself to the necessity to stay perpetually on top, in control. But he would not flinch, yielded to Charles' demand, asked only that the clause be not written into the treaty but remain a verbal undertaking. Doubtless he hoped to be able slowly to persuade Parliament to accept it. The King agreed; a draft of the preliminary treaty was signed.

Joy abounding spread through the land: Anjou granted its princess one and a half tenths of its yearly revenue for her wedding and the Estates voted a subsidy of 33,000 *livres*. Margaret had already been told that she was to exchange the hope of wearing a worthless imperial crown for a royal one which was still considered to be one of the greatest in Europe. At the time she was living at Angers with her mother; but now, informed of the conclusion of an agreement with England, the two ladies set out for Tours.

What dreams must, during that short journey, have filled the mind of the fourteen-year-old girl now promised so glorious a future! Fears of the unknown world she was about to be plunged into had but a secondary place. Even the feeling aroused by the thought that she would soon be dominating the haughtiest nobility in Europe, and enjoying the magnificence of an Eleanor, an Isabel, a Philippa after the indifferently gilded mediocrity of her early years, did not prevail in her mind. Very much her mother's daughter and true heiress of her grandmother, Margaret was passionately interested in public business. Yolande had bequeathed her a love of France and her youthful heart beat high at the idea that she was to become the means of restoring that Kingdom; and that the two mighty enemies, reconciled at last for love of her, were now to inaugurate an age of gentleness and peace to succeed the age of ferocity just ending. A new epoch was beginning; Margaret swore an oath to herself that her name would appear among those of its makers.

Isabel of Lorraine took up residence in the abbey of Beaumont-les-Tours, and there Suffolk hastened to pay his respects to his master's betrothed. He had first a few moments talk with the Queen of Sicily alone, and then Margaret was introduced to him. What was their first impression of each other, these two people whose names were to be for ever linked together by posterity?

The princess was precociously mature, already sure of her power as a woman and skilled in using it; she over-whelmed the very man who had calculated on her beauty and based his hopes on it. And what of her impression of him?

Suffolk was forty-eight. War had been his foster-mother; he was the very model of those barons whose armour we cannot weigh in our hands without amazement. Pride of caste, a ruthless courage and a wish to please which he used as a weapon had shaped a countenance on which military prowess was written in scars.

Such was William de la Pole, who flaunted with

arrogance both the vices and virtues of men of his kind: heroism on occasion, cruelty, ambition, contempt for scruples, chivalry. His self-confidence, his physical well-being and his smile gave him a semblance, still, of youth.

Shakespeare conceived the meeting between the Earl and Margaret as a romantic encounter during which they fell irresistibly in love. Shakespeare detested 'the French-woman', but the evidence does seem to indicate that these two people actually were fascinated with one another.

On 22 May 1444, the Treaty inaugurating the truce which was to last until 1 April 1446 was solemnly agreed, and on the following day the church bells of Saint Martin of Tours pealed out for the betrothal. In honour of these great events, the court did its best to revive the celebrated splendours of the Hôtel Saint-Pol in Queen Isabeau's day. The French gentlemen and the English Lords rivalled each other in brocades, splendid ornaments of dress, and jewelled swords. From the four corners of the realm gentry and commons flocked to see the procession cross the square before the church. At its head came the Kings of France and Sicily, then, in order of precedence, the Duke of Brittany, the Duke of Calabria, the Duke of Alençon, Constable de Richemont, the Count of Vendôme, the Count of Saint-Pol, the Queen of France and Madame Isabelle of Lorraine; the Dauphine Margaret of Scotland, and the Duchess of Calabria; the Dauphin Louis, walking alone and surly; and finally Charles of Anjou, Count of Maine, leading his niece Margaret by the hand.

Led up to Charles, the princess sank into a deep curtsy. The King raised her and led her to the Papal Legate, Mgr Pierre de Mont-Dieu, Bishop of Brescia, who was to officiate. The prelate then read out the provisional dispensation from the Pope granting the cousins licence to wed despite their kinship. Whether as a result of mere administrative slowness, or for some political reason, the proper dispensation was not delivered until a year later.

The ring was placed on Margaret's finger, and organ and choir added harmony to spectacle.

Thereafter at the abbey of Saint-Julien, where the assembled notabilities betook themselves, the feast was prolonged, in the words of a contemporary account, 'until an untimely hour.' On Charles VII's orders all the honours due to the Queen of England were paid to Margaret. Pies as tall as towers opened to reveal two giants carrying trees covered with monstrous fruits; camels advanced carrying 'castles' in which men-at-arms fought mock battles. Innumerable barrels of wine were broached for the common people; alms were distributed among the poor. In short no man was left in doubt of the triumph of love over the dogs of war.

The date for the wedding having been fixed for the following spring, Suffolk returned to England to defend the outcome of his mission. Margaret had a whole year in which to foster her bewitching dreams.

This term spent at Charles's court counted among the happiest periods of her life. The princess was given a taste of the sweets of royalty without knowing anything of its bitterness. The young lords—Beauvau, Laval, Vendôme, Bourbon—flattered and made much of her, and she received their attentions gracefully. She was said to have a secret favourite in Pierre de Brézé, the Seneschal of Poitou.

De Brézé was a giant of a man, but as celebrated for his subtle mind as for his powerful muscles; and despite his youth his official functions were virtually those of prime minister. Almost fanatical in his devotion to the King, he worked hard and persistently to help him deserve the high-sounding epithet of 'Victorious'. Still, he never forgot that by birth he was a vassal of René of Anjou and he was deeply attached to his liege lord's family. And this was reason enough to make him the advocate, in Council, of any proposal likely to be of advantage to the Queen of

England. Perhaps the princess's charm should have some credit for such devoted loyalty. De Brézé called himself her *'chevalier servant'*, and carried her colours in the lists. And Margaret was moved, disturbed, proud of her power over this matchless knight. They vowed to preserve their affection for each other inviolate, however widely space and time should separate them.

It may have been that her mentors, using foresight, should have cut short the girl's all too agreeable residence at the French court. There was a risk that Henry VI's future Queen might retain a dangerous measure of affection for her uncle and his friends.

Meanwhile, the town of Metz rose in rebellion against King René. The citizens complained of the excessive burden of taxation. In the second place they had advanced money to help their suzerain pay his ransom, and complained that the interest on their loans was not being paid. As for the principal, it was best forgotten.

Secretly sustained by the Vaudemonts and even by the Duke of Burgundy, this movement grew, threatening to spread throughout the Duchy. But Charles VII considered that his brother-in-law's interests were identical with his own. He had at command a large army, 30,000 men whom the truce had condemned to an enforced idleness which could become dangerous. Without hesitation, he marched on Lorraine, recalled Toul and Verdun, both hesitating on the brink of revolt, to their duty, and laid siege to Metz. The city was still resisting when the English ambassadors disembarked in France again. Suffolk, newly made a marquis, was this time accompanied by his wife and a numerous suite which included the Earls of Salisbury and Shrewsbury and the lovely Alice Chaucer, Duchess of Somerset; in short, the fine flower of the anti-Gloucester faction of the nobility.

Queen Isabel was anxious to take advantage of these circumstances to marry her daughter in her own beloved

Lorraine whither she had returned after an absence of ten years. So it was decided that the wedding would take place in Nancy. On 3 March 1445 Metz capitulated; magnanimously, the victor exacted no vengeance: the city was required only to agree to regard the King of Sicily's debt to the citizens as settled. Relieved by this means of the burden of his debt, René applied himself to demonstrating —for the honour of his House—that he could flaunt a magnificence quite equal to his brother-in-law's or that of his cousin of Burgundy.

Never had the town of Nancy been host to so splendid and princely a company: all the great feudatories, the representatives of foreign princes, the cream of Europe's nobility crowded cheek by jowl in its beflagged and bedecked streets. If the French, transported by the results of their recovery and revenge, were light-hearted, the English, with the possible exception of Salisbury, were no less so at the triumph of their faction's policy, their coming to power in Margaret's person.

Escorted by Bertrand de Beauvau, Sire of Précigny, Alain Lequeu, Archdeacon of Angers, and Messire Moreau, Treasurer of Anjou, the princess reached Nancy where the cheering dazed her with the heady stuff of popularity; if she had ever doubted her mission she did so no longer.

Her wedding dress was of white satin sewn with silver and gold marguerites. Marguerites were everywhere, scattered underfoot, engraved in the metal of shields, embroidered on the velvet of cloaks and the satin of banners. Flemish tapestries hung from the balconies, church bells pealed joyously, and the sway and surge of the crowd was topped by hennins rocking like sails on a sea swell. Many a gentleman flaunted his whole fortune on his person in gold chains, jewelled hilts and glittering caparisons.

Magnificant chargers carried Charles, a Charles in love,

rejuvenated, and for this occasion unfaithful to the smaller horses he preferred; carried René bathed in carefree, thoughtless happiness, his son John of Calabria, and all the cohort of great feudal chiefs from which only Philip of Burgundy was absent; carried the Dauphin Louis, alone and brooding as ever; and—Agnes Sorel, as over-whelmed with adulation as even the heroine of the day herself. After the chargers came the great decorated carts radiant with Marie of Anjou's sweet smile, the bold smile of Isabel of Lorraine, and the touching, sad smile of the Dauphine, Margaret of Scotland.

Suffolk met the princess on the Cathedral threshold. They entered side by side to the singing of hymns and there Mgr Louis d'Harancourt, Bishop of Toul, joined solemnly before God and men, Henry of Lancaster, King of France and England, Lord of Ireland, Duke of Guyenne and Normandy, to Margaret of Anjou, Princess of Sicily, Jerusalem, Cyprus, Majorca, Provence and Lorraine. The contract, signed on the eve of the wedding day, had specified that by way of dowry the king surrendered to his daughter his claim to Majorca and Minorca . . . Henry VI was at liberty to conquer the islands if he could.

The wedding feast lasted a week; there were banquets, miracle plays, the singing of minstrels, above all jousting presided over and managed by René with meticulous zeal, and the renown of which was to echo down the centuries. Even Charles himself entered the lists, and the nobles disputed for the honour of breaking a lance dedicated to Margaret. Many distinguished themselves on that day, but by general consent it was Pierre de Brézé who bore off the palm. On the last day Agnes Sorel cantered round the lists wearing silver armour encrusted with precious stones.

The end of these rejoicings marked the turning point in Margaret's life—divorce from her country and her family; departure for a mysterious land full of hopes and pitfalls.

Already imbued with a sense of her duty, the girl set out for England dry-eyed and with a smile. More than 1,500 people composed her train. Two leagues from Nancy Charles VII was the first to take leave of her: he 'commended her to God' and embraced her lovingly. That royal caress released an avalanche of presentiments in the poor child; it was as if her future, bloody and terrible, appeared suddenly before her eyes. She wept copiously and could not for some considerable time be consoled. At last uncle and niece parted; they were never to set eyes on each other again.

At Bar-le-Duc Margaret took leave of her parents. Thereafter, of the French, only John, Duke of Calabria and the Duke of Alençon, and their people, remained at her side.

On 16 March the princess and her train reached Paris. To welcome their august visitor, the capital had masked its ruins; through a great concourse of cheering people the princess made her way to Notre Dame where the Archbishop supported by the Cathedral Chapter awaited her. A high mass was sung in her honour, and she was presented with relics from the Treasury.

At Saint-Denis her brother left her, having handed her over officially to the King of England's representative. Suffolk, at this trying moment, was the essence of a sympathetic tact so remarkable that Margaret never forgot it and her gratitude strengthened her early feeling for the English Ambassador.

She was impulsive and downright, judging people instantly, deciding they were either all black or all white, sticking obstinately to her judgements which were only strengthened by contradiction. Thus from that time Suffolk became both the wisest and most devoted of her friends, and she put all her confidence in him. Her insight did not mislead her in one respect: the Marquis was attached to her; but it was the attachment of a partisan seeking an alliance, not that of a disinterested councillor of a child queen.

Thus, Suffolk did not fail, in painting a picture of the English court for Margaret, to do so in colours which matched his own political interests. Before they had reached Normandy the young Queen had already conceived a filial respect for Cardinal Beaufort of Winchester, and a strong aversion to Gloucester and his friends.

At Mantes they boarded ships to reach Rouen, capital of the English possessions in northern France, by water. As soon as Margaret's train came within sight of the city walls, cannon thundered a salute, church bells pealed, and six hundred archers marched out escorting Richard Plantagenet, Duke of York, and Regent of France, come to make his bow to his sovereign's wife.

Margaret already knew this prince by repute, knew him to be thirty-four years old, proud of his rank, his imposing presence and his worth, and bent from youth on winning himself popularity. She knew his double descent from Edward III—through his mother, Lady Mortimer, daughter of the Duke of Clarence, *second* son of the victor of Crécy; and through his grandfather, the fourth son of the same illustrious monarch.* She knew, furthermore, that his father, the Earl of Cambridge, had paid for his plotting with his head and how Richard himself had been reinstated in the dignities and honours of his ancestors, the Duke of York, at Gloucester's instigation, and then appointed to the post which was the most fertile in glory but also in perils, that of Regent of France.

The tacit condition on which Richard was taken back into grace was absolute and eternal silence touching the nature of his kinship with the Mortimers. For the House of Lancaster, reigning since the deposition of Richard II derived only from Edward III's *third* son; and there is no Salic Law in England . . .

* See genealogical tables at the end of this book.

Brought face to face, the new cousins sought to please each other. But their effusive speeches remained merely diplomatic, and failed to establish any strong current of mutual liking. It may have been that Suffolk's views had left Margaret unable to trust any protégé of Gloucester's; and that it was not pleasant for Richard to behold the mother-to-be of a Prince of Wales who must stand for ever between himself and any hope of the throne. It may even be that both had presentiments of the superhuman suffering which each was to inflict on the other.

Behind the Duke came a superb palfrey covered with 'crimson and gold velvet sewn with golden roses', led by a page, Henry VI's present to his bride; then a cart carrying Lady Talbot and the Countess of Salisbury in ceremonial dress; and finally numerous gentlemen recently landed in Harfleur. The banquet served in Rouen's hôtel de ville had both the magnificence and the cordiality proper to the occasion.

Margaret did not stay long in the ancient Norman city. Yet long enough to sense the heartbeat of an heroic people resentful of their servitude and still full of tragic memories of the siege in 1419. England's new Queen was moved less by anger with these intransigent and untameable subjects than—as a French princess—she was touched by such loyalty to their old masters. York, who kept a watchful eye on her, did not miss the point and expressed a certain uneasiness about it to some of the noble lords composing his entourage. That uneasiness seemed, however, to express itself with something not unlike satisfaction.

The *Cock Johan*, of Cherboug, Thomas Adam, master, was ready to carry Margaret to her kingdom. When she set sail, the horizon was dark and the sea stormy, and as the ship drew nearer to the English coast the storm got worse, as if to bar her passage. Soon it became a tempest indeed, unleashing a gale of wind and lashing up the waves with fury. Mountains of water crashed down upon the ship which alternately dived into watery gulfs, and then pointed her bows at the lowering heavens. The sails were torn to shreds, the mast crashed down, fractured, on the deck, and the standard, on which the leopards of England were rampant with such pride among the lilies of France, was transformed into a grey rag; meanwhile the passengers were preparing their souls to appear before the Judgement Seat of God.

In Margaret's ears and those of her ladies, the elements were howling threats which were also warnings. As in a Homeric storm, rival gods strove against each other; those hostile to the princess encouraging the sailors and keeping the ship afloat, while those friendly to her united to keep her from reaching the shore which must be her bane. More than once, shipwreck came near to being her soul's salvation. But the hostile gods were bent on her tragic destiny; and they triumphed, for on 9 April the royal ship, a mastless hulk, was beached near Porchester.

Still the storm did not abate. The gale tore up trees, ripped the roofs from cottages, and driving the sea inland turned miles of coastline into a vast marsh. Sick and dishevelled, her clothes in rags, Margaret set foot in her new country. No welcome awaited her. The mayor and notables of Porchester, hastening to do their best, had to pile carpets on the ground to enable her to approach. But the tempest seemed still set on barring her way, and she had to take refuge in a wretched cottage, where she fainted.

Every violent gust of wind threatened to tear the hovel apart and the rain beat savagely at roof and walls . . .

Such was England's greeting to her Queen.

# The Plantagenet Family

Husband and wife met at Southampton on Wednesday, 14 April 1445. Henry had been consumed by impatience for this moment for months. Fired with gratitude at finding the princess so completely as his imagination had pictured her, he experienced one of those powerful surges of feeling by which shy and timid men are sometimes carried away.

Henry was twenty-three; his face had a melancholy beauty lit by ineffably gentle eyes, full of dreams and secret thoughts and feelings. More or less sickly, indifferent to his appearance, completely free from arrogance and even pride, he seemed a frail creature, the least regal of all his court of tall, strapping noblemen. The impressiveness of this prince was of a different order: it was in the radiance of a goodness and a humanity which were prodigiously rare in that harsh and brutal century. Margaret was far from insensible to it; from the moment of their meeting she conceived a sort of affectionate respect for her husband's character which nothing was ever to diminish.

Conceived without love and burdened with a terrible heredity—his paternal grandfather Henry IV was a leper, his maternal grandfather Charles VI of France, mad—he was born puny and slow-minded. Separated from his

mother in infancy, he was given as tutor the terrible
Beauchamp, Earl of Warwick, who had had the Maid
burnt at the stake. Cantankerous and pitiless in devotion
to his duty, Warwick tried to extirpate the most trifling
flaws in his nephew, whose affectionate and somewhat
fearful nature he entirely failed to understand. He imposed
a ferocious discipline on the boy who, for ever terrified of
doing the wrong thing, withdrew into himself, became
silent, unsociable and at last sought refuge in a bewildered,
pitiful devoutness. In an age when a man's merit was
measured by his physical strength and skill, moreover,
Henry knew himself to be too sickly and feeble ever to
shine. This knowledge increased his timidity and he
became as averse to public ceremonies of all kinds as to
warlike games. The King had all the virtues of a good
monk—goodness, chastity, love of study, forgetfulness of
injuries; he had neither pride, nor anger, nor love of
money. He dismissed from the court a lady who had
flattered herself that she would show him what the pleasures of the flesh meant. Henry's nobles beheld and
marvelled at this gentle scion of the most savage family
of conquerors spawned in Europe since the barbarian
invasions.

At once Angevin, Norman and Aquitanian, with a tiny
admixture of English blood—from William the Conqueror
to Edward IV only the Black Prince and Henry IV married
English women—the Plantagenets derived from three
families in which parricide was, by all accounts, an
ancient tradition and a constantly observed one. As
Angevins they descended from the Counts Fouques,
compared with whom the House of Atreus appears
positively timorous. As Normans they counted among
their ancestors not only the formidable Conqueror himself, but that Henry Beauclerc who had his brother's eyes
put out. As Aquitanians they inherited the furious passions of Eleanor of Aquitaine. Finally, Isabel of France had

bequeathed them the calculating cruelty of her father Philip the Fair.*

The very reverse of the Capets, who were bigots, avaricious, friends of the humble and died in their beds, the Plantagenets had filled the world with the clamour of their quarrels, ransomed their vassals, defied the Holy See, assassinated bishops, flaunted an immorality which would have led ordinary mortals to be burnt at the stake.†And most of them came to a violent or at least dramatic end.

In France, where the great barons had a dangerous strength, king and people had early combined to resist them. In England, on the other hand, the all-powerful sovereign had to face an alliance of Barons and Commons. The Magna Carta, and later the Provisions of Oxford, so limited the royal power as to make it almost constitutional. Thanks to the prestige of his victories Edward III was able to revive that power for a while. But then Richard II's excesses, and the advent of the Lancastrians whose usurpation made them dependent on Parliament and the Clergy, called the whole matter in question again. Henry IV reigned under tutelage. The conquest of France enabled Henry V to reign untramelled. But just because this authority derived from victory, it was apt to crumble away when a wind of misfortune began to blow. Henry VI's only effective weapon was the memory of his father; for the rest, his many virtues did him nothing but disservice. For a prince, a horror of blood-letting, tolerance, and an inability to believe evil are so many stumbling blocks to bring about his fall.

Suffolk had told Margaret: 'The King must be defended.' And the girl, the fifteen-year-old Queen, was all readiness,

---

* She was the instigator of the murder of her husband Edward II who, it is said, was impaled on a spit so that his body would show no outward sign of violence.

† Henry II raped his son's betrothed; the girl was not yet nubile.

all joyful eagerness to bring her energy, her valiant spirit to the aid of the child-like King whose qualities of soul made him so dangerously vulnerable: had not her mother, Isabel, delighted in doing battle for her frivolous husband?

Gloucester she received icily; Beaufort, the Cardinal, with affectionate respect. The difference did not pass unnoticed.

Despite her prepossessions, Gloucester must have hoped that the Queen would be neutral and that, because of her youth, he would be able to make an impression on her. Now he found her bristling with antagonism; and furthermore much too seductive, much too charming to be anything but a dangerous enemy. From that moment he made up his mind to fight. As for Margaret, she had taken sides, and by so doing chosen the road the reign must take; even had she wanted to, she could not have changed it.

On 22 April 1445 the royal pair received a nuptial blessing in Tichfield Abbey and there they spent their wedding night.

Was it Henry who aroused in his wife, who had certainly been without prior initiation, those senses which were, in the Valois, so powerfully demanding? It would be overbold to assert as much. But certain it is that she was grateful to him for a gentleness, a want of selfishness, even an ingenuous awkwardness thanks to which any idea she might well have had of an imperious master, vanished for ever. As for the King, he awoke next morning as wildly in love as any man in his kingdom, and his wife's slave.

They had to wait until 28 May for their ceremonial entry into London. The pretext for this delay was that the City must have time to prepare a fitting reception; the real reason was Parliament's reluctance to vote the necessary credits. The gossips, on the other hand, were saying that in any case it would take that much time to make the

5   Philip the Good, Duke of Burgundy, and his son Charles the Rash; anonymous
    pen-drawing (*Paris, Bibliothèque Nationale, Receuil d'Arras: Giraudon*)

6 The coronation of Henry VI, from *Anciennes Chroniques d' Angleterre* by Jean de Wavrin (*Paris, Bibliothèque Nationale Ms. fr. 83 fol. 105 : Giraudon*)

7 Effigy of Cardinal Beaufort in his Chantry at Winchester Cathedral (*Edwin Smith*)

Portrait of Henry VI by an unknown artist (*London, National Portrait Gallery*)

9   Margaret of Anjou (*Paris, Bibliothèque Nationale, Cabinet des Estampes: R. Lalance*)

Queen's dresses; Her Highness had landed with hardly any underwear, let alone ceremonial robes.

Henry, as a rule so economical, wanted to dazzle his wife, to display something of that gorgeous splendour with which the Plantagenets were wont to mortify the close-fisted, almost bourgeois, Capetian Court. He got his way with Parliament at last, and incidentally did not hesitate to pledge his own property to the same end. It was thanks to his perseverance that the young Queen saw a capital dressed over all in marguerites, with triumphal arches over every street and fountains of ale and malmsey at every cross-roads. Ladies dressed allegorically—as Peace, as Grace, as the cardinal Virtues, made their reverences. A Saint Margaret surrounded by the Foolish and Wise Virgins, bade her welcome. In the principal squares of the city, miracle plays enacted scenes from the Bible. With keen curiosity Margaret looked on the city, already enormous and noisy with a manifold and passionate life. Nothing she had ever seen had prepared her for such a spectacle; had she been thirty years older she would have been reminded of the Paris of the *Cabochiens*.*

Long since victorious over her rivals, London, whose suburbs already extended beyond Temple Bar, considered herself to be the very heart of England. Proud of her ancient buildings and monuments, of her freedom and franchises, of her opulence, of old calamities valiantly lived through, the City's burgesses were powerful, organized and jealous of their rights, its populace jingoistic and easily roused to violence. From the dockside mob to the Aldermen, every man had his own political opinion, his chosen leader, and his particular grudge, and bloody brawls between contending factions were common in the streets.

* Caboche, a Parisien butcher, headed a Burgundian faction in Paris, which attempted some reforms.

Blind prejudice, always ready to fly to arms, arrogance of the *civis romanus* order, and a taste for brawling and rapine—such were the attributes of the Londoners which enabled the lords, both temporal and spiritual, to recruit turbulent partisans and frequently enabled them to confront the government with a *fait accompli*.

The richer classes were more or less sympathetic to Cardinal Beaufort's policies; but sailors, workmen, soldiers and beggars, the 'rogues and vagabonds', idolized Gloucester. And the Duke had made good use of the time available to him to sow among them suspicion and distrust of 'the Frenchwoman'. Looking questioningly out at the endless rows of faces as she passed among the people, Margaret caught glimpses of the admiration due to her beauty, but no trace of that fervent feeling with which loyal subjects greet a young Queen. And while there were ardent cheers for Henry, the name of Margaret was scarcely heard at all. She was blamed for many things—her father's kingly title was an empty boast; she was poor; her dowry was a ridiculous claim to a remote island; her price had been Maine and Anjou.

'Usually', whispered Gloucester's men among the people, 'Queens of England bring their husbands a rich dowry. Not only hasn't this one a shift to wear, but we've had to buy her—and at what a price!'

Margaret might well have been presented to the people as a symbol of peace, and have had her advent blessed as heralding an era of tranquillity, disarmament and reduced taxation. Thanks to the Lord Protector's manoeuvres she was received as a personification of defeat. Her smile should have been irresistible: instead it evoked the memory of Joan of Arc, of fifteen years of reverses, and the loss of an empire. And English patriotism was roused and irritated.

And besides, had not French princesses always brought their husbands bad luck? Men's minds went back to

Henry II, John Lackland, Edward II, Richard II and even, for that matter, to Henry V who had died so suddenly after his wedding . . .

On 30 May 1445 the Queen was crowned in Westminster Abbey. Wearing the crown with the sceptre in her hand, and with the crimson and ermine cloak over her shoulders, Margaret took her seat on Edward the Confessor's throne and received the homage of the princes of the blood, the great Lords, and other high dignitaries. Her grace, her majestic bearing and the radiance of her youth won her many hearts, even some prejudiced against her. The aged Lord Talbot, England's Achilles, was subjugated completely. And yet—how many reservations were there, what a sum of secret opposition and even latent hatred.

Perceiving this hostility, the young Queen held herself all the straighter, prepared for battle. And if, from time to time, she was touched by uneasiness, even anxiety, she had only to turn her eyes to the ecstatic face of the King and then to Suffolk's serene strength, to smile again, full of confidence . . .

When Margaret had installed herself in Westminster Palace in the Queen's apartments which had been unoccupied for twenty years; when her guard had been formed, her Household appointed and her train of matrons and maids of honour assembled; when she had visited the principal royal residences, Windsor, Coventry, Woodstock and Greenwich; when she had, in fact, had time to understand what henceforth her life was to be like, she was somewhat disconcerted.

However rough French manners might be at that time, they were beginning to be modified by a civilization as yet quite unknown on the other side of the Channel. Many English customs harked back to the patriarchal savagery of an earlier age. In France women had already been freed from the more humiliating servitudes; in England those chains were still intact. Ladies of nobility were still their own housekeepers, first among the castle servants. Food, clothes and even feasts were still wanting in those refinements which frequent contacts with Italy had long since introduced among the Valois. In England a meal was composed of nothing but highly spiced meats, and it was customary for the guests to get drunk thereafter. In jousts—which at Aix or at Nancy had become noble and nobly ordered spectacles—the barons were apt to charge and strike each other with such violence that death was a frequent consequence. To unleash a pack of hounds and hunt some poor wretch over the countryside was taken for an amusing pastime to which one invited one's neighbours.

Ostentatious and loud, in England luxury still had a barbaric look about it. René d'Anjou's pleasant Châteaux, precursors of Renaissance building, astonished the English nobles, still faithful to their great, grim fortress-castles.

Many other things in her new country shocked the young princess, and above all the limitations of royal power. She had been accustomed to regard the King as an emanation of the Divine Will, accountable for his acts only to God. For such was the character of French royalty, far, as yet, from being absolute, but deliberately forgetful of its elective origin and, since the work of Philip the Fair's jurists, bound to Roman law. How very different the French princess found English institutions: the King, indeed, reigned by the grace of God; but he ruled by the grace of the Lords, the Clergy and Parliament.

It was Parliament which particularly offended Margaret —a Parliament the reverse of submissive, enjoying freedom of speech and making use of it, intruding into every kind of business—all this seemed scandalous to a French princess. Since the previous century, this assembly of legislators had been separated into two Houses, that of the Peers; and that of the Commons in which sat the Knights of the shires and the representatives of the boroughs. It was the guarantor of the national liberties; it voted the taxes, it decided who was the legitimate heir to the throne; and moreover it had the prerogative, which to Margaret seemed extreme, of impeaching any royal councillor who appeared to have given the King bad advice. It used its privileges with an independence which was sometimes aggressive and it was not intimidated by even the worst kinds of obstructionism. Under Edward I it had had recourse to a kind of general strike, refusing to find any money for the Crown while the Lords, for their part, had declared themselves no longer bound by their traditional military obligations.

Parliament's intransigence was often in the public interest; unfortunately, given the relative weakness of the central government and the limitations of the power of the Crown, it might also be a product of mere factional prejudice, or even be made the instrument of personal ambitions.

As principal authors and primary beneficiaries of the revolution of 1399, the Clergy had, since that date, enjoyed a virtual omnipotence which they had little by little come to take for granted. Gorged with wealth and honours, and delighted with a monarch whose piety recalled that of Saint Louis, they were all in favour of the *status quo* and a quiet life. They remained almost unruffled even by the great wind of national pride when it blew across the land. Under the despotic hand of Cardinal Beaufort, it was the churchmen who inspired the party in favour of peace—a peace by virtue of which they could get their capital out of an undertaking which seemed most unlikely to pay any more dividends.

Cardinal Kemp, Archbishop of Canterbury; the Bishop of Chichester, who was Lord Chancellor; the Bishops of

Hereford and Salisbury, were all members of the King's Council, and there raised barriers against all Gloucester's projects. But their policy was inspired by wholly selfish motives. Had it not been for Beaufort's iron hand they would readily have lost all interest in public business from the moment they were sure of being able to be left in peace to count their hoards of gold in the tranquility of their abbeys.

The Lords temporal, on the other hand, were, in general, for war.

Very prolific, ready for any sacrifice where the interest of their House was concerned, the great families, usually descendants of William the Conqueror's lieutenants, formed wide networks across the shires; networks whose mesh was strong and in which the King or his friends often found themselves caught. Their mighty fortresses, bidding defiance to their sovereign lord, ensured their security and enabled them to maintain a corps of followers who were blindly devoted to them and made them wellnigh invulnerable, unless they could be caught off their guard.

The nobles very early had had the good sense to accept the idea that all men were equal before the law. Consequently they were not hated by the burgesses, who often sat cheek by jowl with their younger sons in the House of Commons. And this again was a source of strength.

The Percys, the Nevilles, the Beauchamps, the Cliffords and the Stanleys and a score of others could raise private armies. Every great lord had his following, his livery, a rout of servants and men-at-arms often numbered by hundreds, and serving both as a body-guard and an instrument of intimidation. These liveries filled London with their misdeeds and no man, not even an Alderman, dared touch one of those ruffians without running the risk of having to answer for it to the noble whose arms the fellow bore.

Arrogant to the point of insanity, quarrelsome, quick

tempered, greedy, fierce, and very touchy, these Lords found in warfare an outlet for their passions and an employment admirably designed to make use of their worst qualities. Peace, which left them with nothing to do, at a loss, automatically inclined them to start a quarrel of some kind. And this inclination was all the stronger after the humiliation of a defeat following such a series of famous victories. Dominated by a fury which must make them easy meat for the first tolerably clever leader that offered, they needed a sacrificial victim, a scapegoat.

Being a good grand-daughter of Yolande, Margaret immediately realized that the dangers of such a state of mind could be dealt with only by an inflexible authority. But was the King capable of exercising such authority?

Henry VI was as much of an enigma to his wife as to his people. Utterly inaccessible to the feelings of his entourage, he seemed to be living not only out of his time but above all out of his circumstances. There were already people muttering that he was not fit to wear a crown; the fact is that the crown was not worthy of him. His physical weakness, his devoutness, his disgust with excesses of the table, had emancipated him from the brutal passions which were the very life of the full-blooded men among whom he had to live. Even his religion, all gentleness and idealism, seemed strange to his Court, whose own religion was marred by a ferocious fanaticism. More at ease dreaming than in action, he loved justice and peace above all things. He relieved the unfortunate, provided care for the sick, teaching for children; and his charity was legendary.

'A saint!' declared the devout.

His broad culture—his clerkly erudition irritated his nobles—was not the least of the eccentricities which made men accuse him of singularity. Not only did Henry apply himself to study; he tried to force other people to imitate him—for example by founding Eton College for poor scholars. It was as if some fairy with a sense of irony had given him, at birth, gifts which were of no use to him, above all a kind of mystical clear-sightedness which made him despise the vain ambitions of wordly men. If this grandson of the mad Charles VI of France was inclined to seem strange in his ways it was because he moved wide-eyed through a world of dreams and even, from time to time, attained a condition of mystical ecstacy. What did the futile wordly cares of his Councillors matter to such a man? To govern a country was an odious task not only because it exposed the ruler to the necessity of committing countless sins, but because Henry, out of touch and sympathy with his own kind, was shy and difficult when he had to deal with them, and hated their intrigues and their hypocrisy.

He was considered to be simple-minded. But the sound instincts of the common people led them to venerate him, and even to believe that he had the power to work miracles.

Margaret, bursting with young, ardent life, might well have despised a husband who was so little like the heroes of chivalrous romances. That, on the contrary, she realized his high moral worth, understood his poetry, respected his touchy modesty, shows that she had rare qualities of heart and mind. The young Queen very soon conceived an agressive, protective affection for him—a feeling which, perhaps, had more of tenderness than passion in it, but which may, for that very reason, have been all the more tenacious. As for Henry, he adored her; and far from imposing his will on hers, wanted nothing better than to obey her. But this meant that she must seek the guide she needed elsewhere. In the royal family? Gloucester, the uncle and the heir presumptive, showed an increasing hostility every day that passed.

Leader of the malcontents, eaten up with mortification at the loss of his power and his wife's condemnation, harassed by the attacks of a disease due to his debauchery, he flaunted his embittered arrogance everywhere. His enormous livery, his vassals and partisans, composed a turbulent and aggressive court. And when he rode through the streets of London, cheered by the mob, it seemed to him and his courtiers that he was the real master of England. His magnificence easily eclipsed that of a King who was as ignorant of fashion as he was indifferent to it; and who was hostile to ostentatious display. But the contrast between these appearances and the reality, served only further to sour his temper. To dull his feelings he plunged into almost daily orgies which greatly shocked his nephew; and the bishops believed he was brooding on some dark design.

Muddle-headed, quarrelsome and ambitious, the Duke was not an evil man at heart, nor was he capable of coldly plotting revenge. But unfortunately the loose, noisy ranting of his 'court' easily went to his head and led him to toy with a score of different plots and plans whose realization he never seriously envisaged.

Margaret was aware of his hatred of France, of his opposition to her marriage and of the treacherous rumours spread abroad by his friends. She loathed him, made a virtue of it, and never missed a chance of wounding his pride and susceptibilities, whether in word or deed.

It seems that at one time she thought of turning to Richard of York. Although he was Regent of France the truce enabled him to spend much of his time at Court, involved in intrigues with his brother-in-law, Salisbury, chief of the formidable Neville family. No man knew exactly what Richard, great-grandson of Edward III, had in mind; but he could not forget his claim to the throne and he worked patiently and quietly at recalling it to the memories of the nobility in general. He had undeniable qualities of mind and person, and both his courage and his pleasing manners made him popular. But Margaret soon sensed that he was too intent on his own personal interest and too apt to involve himself in obscure and devious plans to be of use to her. Besides, she liked Somerset, Richard's sworn enemy, the better of the two: the two cousins in their mutual hostility revived the old strife between Gloucester and the Cardinal.

Edmund, second Duke of Somerset, represented the older branch of the Beaufort family, issue of John of Lancaster's third marriage to Catherine Swynford. His French campaigns had earned him some renown, but he was not liked by the people. In his forties, he was an epicure, with agreeable manners and a handsome person, a man imperturbably sure of himself. Not even the most outrageous flattery or toadying ever surprised him. Unfortunately he had neither the gift nor the energy to be the sort of great man he assumed himself to be. But, foreseeing that the Queen must soon have great influence, he had made a point of making much of her as soon as she came upon the scene; Margaret was grateful to him, yet she had few illusions about the real value of his advice. And that left her with only one possible councillor among the princes of the blood: the Cardinal.

Seventy-eight years crowded with passions, battles, and crimes had done nothing to calm that 'savage pride' which Shakespeare attributes to him, nor had they slaked his thirst for power. They had done no more indeed, than soften and smooth his bearing and address, so conferring upon him something of the serene majesty which becomes a prince of the Church. The old man treated the young Queen with paternal affection and Margaret congratulated herself on having met with so venerable an elder in her new country. What more reliable mentor could she have hoped to find than an affectionate prelate devoted to the King, and moreover one whose great age must surely be a guarantee of genuine disinterestedness? Furthermore it was he who had chosen poor René of Anjou's daughter to reconcile the two kingdoms from among the many he might have preferred. Was it not the least she could do to work for the success of his policy? So, uncle and niece became intimate friends; Margaret had her own apartments, which the Cardinal had had especially prepared for her, at Latham, his house; and she was often there. Deprived of the amusements proper to her youth, at a loss in a court where manners were coarse and tempers bad, she fell back on her interest in public business: her long talks with the eloquent, wheedling old Cardinal were an oasis of recreation in the desert of insipid and tedious ritual which constituted her working life.

And Beaufort took advantage of them to initiate her into State secrets and lay down what her course of behaviour should be: the Queen must breathe some of her own life and energy into the King, guard him, smooth his path to the right councillors; for the rest she should defend the cause of peace with all her might, and do her best to thwart the plans of the faction-leaders. What, alas, he omitted to teach his pupil were impartiality, tolerance and the art of always leaving an enemy the chance to change sides.

Margaret's natural boldness, and the obstinate strength of her convictions predisposed her to take the fiery old man's lessons to heart. And during her visits to Latham she frequently met Suffolk and continued to like and admire him as much as ever. The mature man and the girl Queen understood each other remarkably well; and as for him, the loving respect, the near veneration he treated her with far surpassed what might be required by mere loyalty.

In Suffolk's robust and soldierly presence, she felt safe; and could give expression to a confiding friendship of a kind which her all-too-perfect husband could not inspire.

The rumour of their friendship spread all the more swiftly because it had never occurred to her proud Angevin spirit that she might do well to conceal it. Already preferred to a number of important offices, her friend was now made a duke. Gloucester's partisans were quite ready to make the most of this state of affairs. Soon there was not a tavern loafer or apprentice in all London who was not sure that Suffolk was the Queen's lover.

# Games for Princes

Henry's marriage had brought him the first happiness he had known. His beloved surpassed in grace and beauty all the princesses of the time; and her mind, open and sensitive to every intellectual impression, enabled the young King to go on a thousand of those enchanting journeys through cloud-cuckoo-land which were his delight. Within a few months Margaret had lightened and embellished his gloomy castles, made fashions in clothes gayer and more delicate, introduced an element of fancy into life at the Court. When Henry walked beside the sweet witch who had wrought these wonders, under Windsor's leafy trees or in Woodstock's maze, while making a thousand plans for the happiness of mankind, he gave thanks to Heaven for his happiness. Unfortunately, the business of politics would not be dismissed.

On 13 July 1445 an important French embassy arrived in London. It included, as Charles VII's representatives, Mgr Louis de Bourbon, Count of Vendôme; Juvénal des Ursins, Archbishop of Reims; Guy, Lord of Laval; and, as King René's envoys, the Sire de Sable and the Sire de Tucé. Their business was to claim the cession of Maine which had been verbally promised by Suffolk.

Henry prevaricated. For his part there was nothing he so ardently wished for as peace, and he was more or less prepared to buy it. But he had to reckon with a very tough and uncompromising opposition. The Ambassadors, however, were accommodating. All they claimed was the usufruct of the county for René's brother, Charles of Anjou, during his lifetime only. And, by way of some indemnity for England, Charles VII would pay her a sum equal to ten years' revenue from Maine.

Nevertheless, the war party raised a terrible outcry. To gain time, Henry made a condition: he must have a twenty year alliance between himself and the House of Anjou. With which meagre booty the negotiators left for France. On 17 October a second delegation composed of Messires Havart and Coussinot arrived in London with instructions from René to accept his son-in-law's offer. But on the English side there seemed no more sign than before of haste to conclude the treaty. It is by no means sure that Beaufort and Suffolk did not wish to be forced into the position of being unable to keep their word.

Margaret became angry. The youthful ardour of her loyalties had no patience with diplomatic subterfuge. Her mission was to bring her two families into agreement and to insist that the undertakings entered into be respected. To the great scandal of the English she begged, implored, wept, raged and opened direct correspondence with her uncle of France in a letter dated 17 December 1445. She got her way, on 22 December Henry extended the truce with France and gave a solemn undertaking to hand over Maine on 30 April 1446 'to please the King of France and at the request of his wife.' This wording filled Margaret's heart with pride, she had shown herself worthy of King Charles' confidence. It did not occur to her that for England, then and later, those words damned her.

30 April came at last and orders were issued to evacuate Maine. Disgusted and furious, the governor of Le Mans refused to obey them; and, infected by his example, other captains copied his disobedience. So great was the people's

joy in England that the Court did not dare openly to
reprove these officers. Margaret was in despair. To soothe
Charles VII she wrote him a particularly affectionate letter
from Windsor on 21 May 1446.

... We have hope, most high and puissant prince, our very dear
uncle, that it will be the pleasure of my said Lord that with
him ... by the Grace of God, we shall effectively see a fruitful
conclusion to the matter of the general peace, that in all worldly
things we desire to be guided by cordial affection ... for the
maintaining and fostering of union and true concord between
you two who are so nearly related in consanguinity ... And do
you always signify to us all things agreeable to you [to be done]
that we may accomplish such as are within our power, joyfully
and with all our heart ...

Again she pleaded with everybody concerned, harassed
the King and his councillors. But this time, to no purpose.
But she was tenacious. She conceived the idea of trying to
find an ally in the war party: she suggested to the Duke of
York that he might marry his son, Edward, Earl of March,
to the Princess Madeleine of France, Charles VII's
daughter. The idea caught on, took shape. Charles was
harassing his niece who tried to calm his impatience:

10 December 1446.
... In that you pray and exhort us perseveringly to hold our
hand towards my most redoubted Lord that on his part he be
still inclined to the benefit of peace, may it please you to know
that in truth we are employed at it and shall be with good heart
so far as it shall be possible ...

And on 17 December 1446 another letter which reads like
self-justification.

... For better pleasure could we not have in this world than to
see appointment of final peace between him and you ... And in
that, at our Lord's pleasure, shall on our part extend our hand

and shall employ ourselves to the utmost of our power in such manner as that in reason you and all other must be content. And as to the matter of the deliverance which you desire of the county of Maine and other things contained in your letters, we hear that my said Lord is writing to you . . . and nevertheless in this, we shall for your pleasure do the best that we can do as we always have done . . .

The Duke of York long delayed writing to the King of France. However on 21 December he did so at last:

With regard to the overtures made touching the treaty of marriage between Madame Madelaine and my eldest son, in truth, most high, excellent and puissant prince, I am of the same mind, desiring that by the Grace of God, the thing be brought to a good and effective conclusion . . .

Nevertheless, this project came to nothing. It may be that Suffolk arranged to prevent it, in order to prevent a dangerous rapprochement between Richard and the Queen. On the other hand it may simply have been lost sight of in the storm which, at this moment in time, broke over the land.

The very air of the Kingdom was becoming unbreathable.

Two years of peace had, by easing economic difficulties, softened men's memories of the miseries of war; all that remained sharp was the humiliation of a deplorable peace at the thought of which even cool heads became heated. Already Englishmen were ceasing to believe in the reality of the defeats suffered from the moment Joan of Arc had appeared on the scene. If the truce of Tours really had almost wiped out the glorious Treaty of Troyes, the fault must lie at the door of traitors who had taken advantage of the King's weakness. And was not the Queen herself encouraging those traitors? Her obstinacy in insisting that

10　Detail from *La Chasse du duc de Bourgogne*, showing Philip the Good, Duke of Burgundy (*Musée de Versailles: Cliché du Service de Documentation Photographique des Musees Nationaux*)

11  View of London from the *Poems of Charles of Orleans* (late fifteenth century)
(*London, British Museum Royal Ms 16F II, fo. 73*)

England give up one of the flowers of the conquest was damning proof of her dark designs. Old England needed a man to restore her greatness; and that man was the good duke Humphrey.

All the malcontents, from the hard-line *revanchards* to the mere fishers in troubled waters, rallied to the erstwhile Lord Protector. A score of times every day the London streets became clamorous with their outcries and brawling as they clashed with the episcopal liveries. But this display of dangerous popularity did not result in the reins of government being restored to Gloucester; they remained firmly clutched in the Cardinal's still powerful hands. Beaufort did not hesitate to remind men of his hephew's follies, of his prevarications, of his fatal passion for Jacqueline of Hainaut, a major cause of English reverses, of his thrusting clumsiness in seeking a crown for himself in the Low Countries, and of his wife's trial and conviction for witchcraft.

Gloucester riposted by recalling the old prelate's violent excesses of temper and temperament, and other abuses: one night Henry V had, thanks to his dog, found a would-be assassin concealed under his bed. The victor of Agincourt had never been in any doubt about who sent the man: Beaufort. Gloucester also accused the old man of encouraging the love affair between Suffolk and the Queen, and of helping them to sell the motherland to the French King. Pamphleteers in his pay revelled in this kind of thing.

The quarrels between York and Somerset were no less violent. Some authors place the famous story of the roses in this period—the story of how friends of the two Dukes were involved in a dispute in the Temple gardens, which ended in York's partisans picking a white rose, while Somerset's chose a red one as their emblem; Margaret is supposed thereafter to have worn a red rose to show her friendship with the Beauforts.

G

Be that as it may, one day in December 1446, Suffolk brought before the Council a villein, William Catour by name, apprentice to Master John Daveys, armourer to the Duke of York. The apprentice accused his master of having uttered seditious words by saying that the crown legitimately belonged to Richard, Duke of York who was being wrongfully kept out of his heritage by Henry of Lancaster. There were plenty of people in England who had entertained this thought; but none had yet expressed it openly in so many words. Consequently feeling ran high and York himself was the first to demand that the man be ruthlessly punished. The armourer, however, denied the charge; and for want of a better system, the judges had recourse to the 'judgement of God' by ordering the accused and his accuser to fight a duel with single-sticks: being base-born, swords were denied them.

The duel took place at Smithfield in the presence of the King, the Queen and the whole Court. Expense had not been spared to make the event impressive. Malevolent gossips were whispering that God would not only pronounce judgement on a criminal but also on the reigning House's title to the throne. The apprentice, being young and active, had little difficulty in flooring his opponent: God having thus pronounced John Daveys guilty, not much time was spent on the rest of his trial; he was hanged, cut down and burnt, in customary style.

This incident, which probably persuaded Margaret to give up her project of marrying the Earl of March to Madeleine of France, made a strong impression on the King's conscience. Often, in the privacy of his oratory, he weighed and brooded on his right to the throne, deeply disturbed by the knowledge that at the root of his title lay a murder. The shade of Richard II, assassinated by Henry's grand-father who became Henry IV, haunted him. It was largely in an attempt to expiate that crime—committed twenty-two years before his birth—that he undertook such harsh penances and lived his life by an almost monastic rule.

And now doubt was added to remorse. By all the rules of dynastic law his cousin, who traced his descent from both the second and fourth sons of Edward III, had a better claim to the throne than the House of Lancaster which derived from Edward's third son. Not another prince living would have troubled himself with such scruples. But for Henry, the very idea of keeping another man out of his rights, and of reigning as a usurper, was a heavy cross to bear. As a good Englishman with a proper respect for forms and customs, he could comfort himself with the idea of *customary right* (*droit d'usage*). He felt that as his father and grand-father had both possessed the crown, and he himself had worn it since childhood, his right was unassailable. Nevertheless, the problem tormented him.

The furies animating his Barons were equally horrifying. All his own efforts in Council were towards reconciling and calming them. The language which Shakespeare puts into his mouth is not merely the product of the poet's literary preoccupations, when Henry addresses his Councillors in such terms as

> Uncles of Gloucester and of Winchester,
> The special watchmen of our English weal,
> I would prevail, if prayers might prevail,
> To join your hearts in love and amity
> O! What a scandal is it to our crown,
> That two such noble peers as ye should jar!
> Believe me, Lords, my tender years can tell
> Civil dissension is a viperous worm,
> That gnaws the bowels of the commonwealth.

> (1 Henry VI, 3.i)

Here it is a child speaking; but as we have said, in his

twenties he was still a child. But alas, his efforts obtained very little result.

Suffolk's ambition being now thoroughly aroused by favour, he conceived a grandiose plan: he would take advantage of the dissension between the princes to make them destroy each other, and thus be left, thanks to the Queen's influence, master of the government. His first move, was to persuade the Cardinal to ruin Gloucester. The old man was beginning to fail, and furious at the idea that after his death his enemy might again seize power, he was not willing to die without having finally destroyed him. It was not difficult to convince Margaret that the Duke was plotting against the King. And, in fact, even if no plot really existed, a plot was entailed by force of circumstances: there were too many people who had founded all their hopes on the former Protector.

An incident, an item of tendentious news, might raise the suburbs at any moment. The Tower and Westminster would be over-run in two hours. Henry and Margaret would be cloistered for life, and Eleanor Cobham, magnificently avenged, would be crowned by Gloucester. This picture painted in lurid colours by Beaufort and Suffolk, roused the young Queen's spirit. She should, could and would defend her husband, and show the conspirators what it meant to be a daughter of Lorraine. She asked Henry to have the Duke arrested. For a long time the King hesitated. He disliked Gloucester because of his dissolute life and above all for his odious treatment of Henry V's widow. Still, he was his nearest kinsman, his one-time tutor. Besides, violence of any kind was so repugnant to him.

Convinced that she was working for the right, Margaret used tears and caresses. What would happen to her if Gloucester carried out his plan, confined his King in a monastery? The answer was not far to seek: look at what he had done to Catherine of Valois.

That was the argument which forced Henry to make up his mind. And once he had done so, Suffolk and Winchester started the wheels turning. They surrounded themselves with men they could trust and who were hostile to the Protector—the Percys, the Cliffords and Owen Tudor, the late Queen Catherine's second husband whom Henry VI had restored to favour. But in London the common people's affection for the Duke of Gloucester made him invulnerable. It was essential to remove him from their protection. This the King did by calling a Parliament at Bury St Edmunds, in Suffolk's own county, where rebellion seemed impossible.

On 10 February 1447 the King and Queen, escorted by a veritable army, opened Parliament in St Edmund's Abbey. All the princes of the blood, the lords temporal and spiritual, the knights of the shires and the borough members were present in full strength. The Archbishop of Canterbury spoke on the subject of peace and good council. Henry's sick, preoccupied air was remarked on. There can be no more tragic fate for a young man burdened with an over-scrupulous conscience than to find himself responsible for a nation's happiness.

The first sitting, devoted to fixing the Queen's jointure, passed off without incident. On the following day Gloucester received an order summoning him to attend upon the King in his room. There was nothing unusual about that and the Duke made his way to the Abbey unescorted, and with no arms but his dress sword.

He found the King with the Queen, the Cardinal and the Dukes of Somerset and Suffolk. Gloucester was hardly inside the room when Suffolk, addressing him angrily, accused him of plotting against the King's person and the safety of the Realm. Moreover, he reproached him for his contempt for the laws of the land, his former maladministration, and the slanders propagated by his means against the Queen's honour. Taken aback, Gloucester defended himself, recalling his former services, the care he had taken of his nephew as a boy, his disinterestedness and his well-known clemency.

The King said not a word, but Margaret jeered, 'The King knows your merits, my Lord,' to which Gloucester replied that towards or against all men he would always remain the first and most faithful of the King's subjects.

He left the room; but as he passed out of the royal antechamber his way was barred by Viscount Beaumont, the Queen's Steward, with a numerous escort of guards.

'In the King's name, my Lord, I arrest you.'

The Duke was about to give way to one of his outbursts of violence when he read, in the faces of the men confronting him, that they were expecting precisely that, waiting for him to give them the excuse to kill him. He quickly regained his self-control, thrust his sword back into the scabard, and confined his protest to declaring his innocence.

The boldness of this *coup* astounded all England and it was realized that henceforth the King's gentleness would be stiffened by a will more manly than his own. Not one of Gloucester's friends dared make a move; while a number of Lords whose loyalty had, at best, been shaky, now hastened to the Court to assure the King of their devotion.

A prisoner he might be, but Gloucester was still redoubtable. Sick and shaking with fever, Cardinal Beaufort had nightmare visions of the Duke being haled triumphantly out of his prison and profaning his old enemy's tomb.

On 23 February, the Duke of Gloucester was found dead in the house where he was confined.

It cannot be denied that he had made bad use of his power; but he did not deserve so cruel an end and, in the event, his death did not strengthen but weakened the Lancastrian cause. All England cried aloud that murder had been done. It was in vain that the physicians recalled the Protector's old sickness and talked learnedly of a paralysis brought on by a seizure; equally in vain that the body was exposed for several days in the great hall of Parliament so that all men could see for themselves that no violence had been done.* Some spoke of poison, others remembered Edward II's horrible death, but all were agreed in damning Suffolk and Margaret—who were probably innocent.

As for Beaufort, he was swiftly approaching his end. Like Mazarin two centuries later, but with even more rage and bitterness, he wandered from room to room of his palace, crying, 'Why should I die, having so much riches: if the whole realm would save my life, I am able either by policy to get it or by riches buy it. Fie, will not death be hired, nor will money do nothing?'†

He continued the strife until his last breath. The Furies stood about his death-bed, conjuring up the ghosts of his victims—Henry V the Valiant, Gloucester athirst for vengeance, men of science burnt for witchcraft, soldiers who had starved to death because of his avarice; and, dominating all the rest of these shades, haloed by the flames of the stake, the terrible spectre of the Maid of Domrémy.

The consolations of religion did nothing to calm the frenzy of his end. On 15 March 1447 the Cardinal died in fury; and no man who beheld the dying rictus could have doubted that he had gone straight to hell and damnation. None wept for him but Margaret, who refused to hear tales of his evil doing, looking upon him as a second father. Time was to reveal that his paternal teaching had not been such as could help her.

* Cf. Hall/Holinshead, 'Some judged him to be strangled, some affirm that an hot spit was put in at his fundament, others write that he was smouldered (smothered) between two featherbeds, and some have affirmed he died of very grief. . . .'     † Holinshead.

With Gloucester and Beaufort out of the way, Suffolk had only York and Somerset to deal with.

Equally ambitious, each thought himself as worthy as the other to rule. But York seemed the more dangerous, and many of the old Protector's partisans—Exeter, Buckingham, Norwich—now looked to him as their chieftain. Married to a Neville, he derived a formidable strength from that powerful family whose power was even now to be doubled by a great marriage. The young son of the Earl of Salisbury, head of the family, was marrying the Beauchamp heiress and thereby becoming Earl of Warwick, lord of countless vassals.

Somerset's vanity and indolence made him, on the other hand, much easier to manage. Besides, Margaret preferred him to his haughty rival. Guided by her advice, that is to say by Suffolk's, Henry VI made Somerset Regent of France; and York Governor of Ireland, an appointment equivalent to honourable exile. Both set out for their posts, the new Regent content, but Richard burning with rage and brooding dark designs.

Suffolk was left master of the field.

# Suffolk's Death

The real reign of Margaret of Anjou began in the spring of 1447. It is disconcerting, to say the least, to think of a seventeen-year-old girl for whom an interest in pretty clothes might have been more appropriate than the charge of public business, resolutely taking up such a crushing burden. One might even be tempted to treat the idea with scepticism, were it not for the fact that her appetite for work and business is attested by irrefutable documentation.

All Henry's official letters, particularly those addressed to the King of France, were doubled by letters from Margaret. The Queen insisted on being kept informed, down to the smallest details, of the progress of all negotiations, the national finances, and the state of the army. She sifted all 'police' reports.

Since the deaths of his uncles, the King had quite lost the ephemeral happiness of the first months of his marriage: at once uxorious and neurotic, he was grateful to his wife for relieving him of duties which he found intolerable. Henry was of the number of those Utopians whose dreams make the real world uninhabitable. It may be that he conceived a scheme of ideal government, precise ideas for establishing that fear of the Lord which is called the beginning of wisdom, the well-being of the poor, and goodwill among men. But since the greed and wickedness of his contemporaries made such work impossible, he preferred to turn altogether away from the world and to forget his disappointment with men among books and in his religious exercises.

Margaret admired her husband's saintliness, and to watch over and ensure his peace and quiet constituted, for her, the most important of her duties. Her principal advisers now were—apart from Suffolk—Cardinal Kemp, Bishop of Chichester; and Lord Say, Suffolk's closest friend.

We possess several of the letters which she wrote in 1447, signed with her own hand. Her writing is firm, the downstrokes vigorous. A strong-willed flourish underlines the broad, open letters of her name, expressive of a frankness which is almost aggressive. A highly developed artistic sensibility can be read in the spacing, and an undeniable highmindedness. But the ruthless crossing of the 'T' is suggestive of an uncompromising and challenging spirit.

Albion the austere should have idolized a Queen who preferred the hard work of government to the pleasures proper to her age. It is a fact that her bold courage and her beauty made fanatical adherents of many men in her entourage. Unhappily, for the majority of the English, she remained *the foreigner*. Gloucester's blood was upon her head, and her affection for Suffolk seemed to justify the worst gossip of her enemies. The more virulent the attacks on the favourite, the more clearly Margaret showed her affection for him. In spite of the nobles who were exasperated by jealousy, of the commons still faithful to the memory of 'good duke Humphrey', and of a Parliament set on a course of deliberate hostility, she kept him by main force at the head of affairs. And she married his son to the Beaufort heiress of the first Duke of Somerset.

In less troubled times the Queen's policy and that of

her ministers would have met with general approval: a lasting peace abroad; at home, restoration of England's former prosperity; encouragement of trade; broadening of education. Henry had founded Eton and King's College, Cambridge. Margaret founded Queen's College, placed under the patronage of Saint Margaret. She sent to the Low Countries and Lyon for skilled craftsmen to improve the woollen industry and establish silk weaving.

In foreign affairs, the question of Maine was still the one stumbling stone on the way to an understanding with France. Charles VII was still persecuting his niece: to borrow an expression which was to be used three centuries later by the Empress Maria-Theresa talking to Mercy d'Argenteau* about Marie-Antoinette, Charles considered Margaret a 'bad payer'.

For Margaret, this was a double penalty; she was wounded in her pride, and also in her desire to make an end of old quarrels. An impartial observer, reading the copious correspondence between her and her uncle during the year 1447, can discern her often touching determination to attain this eminently praiseworthy goal; but an English reader, blinded by patriotic prejudice, could perfectly well—using the same evidence—maintain that she was acting as a French agent. As for the results she obtained, they were not equal to her efforts: pleas and threats alike failed to make any impression whatever on the recalcitrant governor of Le Mans.

Charles, his patience exhausted, reassembled the army which had just returned from a victorious campaign in Switzerland, and in 1448 took the place by storm. The rest of the county offered little or no resistance. There was a roar of anger from England; and the cup of bitterness ran over when Margaret pushed through an agreement by the terms of which Henry undertook to indemnify

* Maria-Theresa's correspondent at the French court of Louis XVI.

English landowners in Maine who were dispossessed by the French victory. The treasury being empty, nobody got a penny. By way of protest, Parliament refused to vote taxes. Brought to bay, Suffolk had recourse to a desperate expedient—selling bishoprics—that alienated the only class in the nation which was still favourable to him.

Cardinal Kemp, Archbishop of Canterbury, and primate since Cardinal Beaufort's death, and the Bishop of Chichester, who was Lord Chancellor, were, however, devoted to the Lancastrian cause and both admired the Queen's courage. Their influence kept a majority of the clergy loyal. But many of the prelates were weary of propping up an edifice which constantly threatened to collapse: and by striking at their interest Suffolk's measure drove them into a hostile neutrality. Then in January 1449, came a cry of alarm from Somerset which brought an impending danger out into the open where all could see it.

The truce was about to expire and the French King seemed by no means disposed to extend it. Since the treaty of Tours his situation had improved whereas Henry's was much worse. Charles had introduced valuable and popular reforms at home, triumphed over the *Praguerie*,* and demonstrated his military strength even as far away as Switzerland. By virtue of a new law ordering the conscription of one archer for every thirty persons of the population, he could put 60,000 men into the field. It was an enormous army for those days: Henry V had conquered France with 24,000 men. His artillery, the work of the brothers Bureau, was the best in Europe. Jacques Coeur had filled his coffers. And finally his ministers and generals, Richemont, Dunois, Brézé, Tancarville had earned him the name of Charles the Well-Served.

* A major rising of Grandees (John V of Britanny, the Duke of Bourbon, Dunois, and the Dauphin Louis), which got its name from contempory troubles in Bohemia.

To this formidable power Normandy could oppose only a small number of soldiers, disaffected because poorly fed and irregularly paid; fortifications in a semi-ruinous state; too few guns; and hardly any reserves. Unless powerful reinforcements could be sent, and sent at once, England's Continental territories were lost. Yet it was in vain that Suffolk read the Regent of France's urgent appeal for help to Parliament. For most members the enemy to destroy was the minister himself.

An Aragonese captain in England's service, whose company had been on garrison duty in Maine, found himself at large in open country as a result of the English evacuation of that county. He asked a number of Norman towns for asylum, but none were willing to share their stores of victuals with newcomers. For a while the Aragonese managed to live off the country by pillage but at last, driven by hunger, he seized and sacked the considerable town of Fougères. Now, Fougères belonged to the Duke of Brittany, ally and vassal of the King of France. Both protested vigorously: in a long memorandum addressed to Somerset, Charles VII recapitulated his complaints against the English; bad faith in carrying out the terms of the Treaty; piracy against the King of Castile's ships—Castile was his ally—and continual brigandage. He demanded the restitution of Fougères and an enormous indemnity—1,600,000 gold crowns, of which the Regent would have had difficulty in finding the first penny. Even had he the means to comply, his fear of Parliament would have prevented him from doing so.

Receiving no indemnity, the French helped themselves: they seized Pont de l'Arche, Verneuil, Valogne, and Upper and Lower Normandy were invaded simultaneously. The whole Duchy seemed a helpless prey. And everybody— even the Duke of Burgundy—was bent on carving himself a piece of it. The war was on again.

For Margaret the blow was a terrible one: her mission,

her policy and her plans were in ruins. She was almost isolated in the midst of a hostile nation which would never do her justice, and yet it lay with her to lead the fight against her father, her uncle and her friends. The French captains were her own former cavaliers: Pierre de Brézé was in command of the vanguard, and René of Anjou rode by Charles' side. And soon other cares distracted her mind even from that torment: every ship which arrived from France brought news of a defeat—Evreux fallen, then Lisieux, Mantes, Louviers, Gournay; Rouen beseiged . . .

Overwhelmed at first, then mad with rage, the people demanded a victim, a man they could hold responsible. They would not, could not, recognize either the immense effort made by France to become once again her old self, or Somerset's incompetence—he had distributed his troops in small parties to defend places whose ruined fortifications were knocked into rubble by Bureau's cannon. No! Normandy had been delivered over to the enemy—by Suffolk.

The Duke could no longer go out into the London streets without an escort. Street boys ran after him singing a macabre song in which his name was mingled with the words of the *De Profundis*.

As for Henry, it is possible that he suffered no less from the defeats inflicted on his army, than from horror at the unleashing of all these hateful passions. 'What manner of man is my uncle of France,' he demanded, naively, 'to cause me so much displeasure?' And they answered him, 'He is a gentle prince, of good council and well spoken, reading better than any other ever read.' And the King sighed, cursing the sombre legacies which set against each other kinsmen who were surely designed to understand and love one another.

The final blow came in October 1449. Besieged in Rouen castle by both the French army and the rebellious citizens, Somerset gave way to the panic terrors of his wife who, with their young children, was at her husband's side; and although he had a numerous garrison under his command, the flower of England's knighthood, even Lord Talbot himself, he capitulated. And what a capitulation! Not to mention a comparatively small pecuniary indemnity—50,000 crowns, he gave up to the French Arques, Dieppe, Caudebec, Lillebonne and Honfleur. Still worse, as a token of good faith, he handed over Talbot, the national hero, as hostage.

And as Honfleur refused to yield, the old soldier, with rage in his heart, was forced to witness his enemies' triumph. 'All pensive and grieved'* he followed Charles' triumphal entry into the Norman capital, saw Harfleur forced by Bureau's cannon despite the December frost, and Honfleur, without hope of relief, open her gates at last.

Upon hearing of this latest disaster, Suffolk made up his mind to a last, supreme effort. Using whatever men he could get, he scraped up an army of 6,000, and entrusted them to a good general—Sir Thomas Kyriel—with orders not to scatter them but to offer the French pitched battle. But it was already too late. Somerset, frantically anxious to exculpate himself by incriminating someone else, wrote to the King accusing Suffolk of having left Normandy without victuals, fortifications and reinforcements. For Parliament, the real culprit, this was a chance too good to miss. The Commons remembered their old privilege of impeaching bad councillors of the sovereign. A supplication 'full of love and affection' was addressed to Henry VI:

In this strange document, the most contradictory things were simultaneously asserted: Suffolk was selling England to the King of France and to *the Queen's father*; he had a castle full of

* *tout pensif et marri.* Jean Chartier.

armaments for the enemy to land in England. And why was he thus summoning the French, the Queen's kinsmen and friends? To *make his own son King*, and overthrow the King and Queen. This seemed logical and well argued. John Bull had not a doubt.*

Margaret jibbed. She would neither admit the validity of a law which could humiliate the monarchy, nor even any need to compromise. She urged the King to use force, and in order to have the same favourable conditions as at the time of Gloucester's arrest, had Parliament summoned to meet in Leicester. Meanwhile, over in Ireland, Richard of York was watching events for the chance he did not intend to miss. Suffolk was not going to escape him.

To intimidate both the Council and the Clergy, chief bulwark of Lancaster, Richard struck hard. The Bishop of Chichester, the Lord Chancellor, was assassinated; and no man dared to seek out his murderers. Terrified, the King's friends were all, suddenly, for temporizing, and Parliament emboldened, refused to meet in Leicester. It was in London that Suffolk had to appear at the Bar of the House.

In vain he pleaded his kinsmen fallen in their country's service, his thirty-four campaigns in France, his wounds, his poverty caused by the payment of an enormous ransom, his attachment to the royal family. Both white and red roses were against him; for York's partisans were bent on opening a way for their leader; and Somerset's on exculpating theirs. To save the Duke's life Margaret conceived an expedient: without waiting for Parliament's verdict, she had the King condemn him to five years banishment. Thus the Queen and her friend had to part. It was a moment charged with feeling. What was, in truth, the nature of the tie which bound them? Shakespeare, at least, had no doubt that they were lovers:

* Michelet. *History of France.*

*Queen Margaret.* O! let me entreat thee, cease! Give me thy hand,
    That I may dew it with my mournful tears;
    Nor let the rain of heaven wet this place,
    To wash away my woeful monuments.
    O! could this kiss be printed in thy hand,
    That thou mightst think upon these by the seal,
    Through whom a thousand sighs are breath'd for thee.
    So, get thee gone, that I may know my grief;
    'Tis but surmis'd whiles thou art standing by,
    As one that surfeits thinking on a want.
    I will repeal thee, or, be well assur'd,
    Adventure to be banished myself;
    And banished I am, if but from thee.
    Go; speak not to me, even now be gone.
    O! Go not yet. Even thus two friends condemn'd
    Embrace and kiss, and take ten thousand leaves,
    Loather a hundred times to part than die,
    Yet now farewell; and farewell life with thee!

                                  (2 Henry VI, 3.ii)

The Duke tried to put new heart into the Queen. They had a last chance, Kyriel's army. Since Bannockburn, 150 years ago, the English had never once suffered defeat in a pitched battle. If Kyriel could force the French to fight, a splendid victory would restore the realm's fortunes and the Queen's friend.

But Suffolk very nearly failed to get out of London at all: a gang of ruffians, among them many professional soldiers who had been bought, were waiting for him in the suburbs. They tried to kidnap him. But the Queen had given him an escort of reliable men. There was a skirmish, men were killed and wounded on both sides, but the Duke got away safe and sound. He reached Ipswich, anxiously watching wind and weather lest it be impossible to put to sea. Meanwhile, Margaret was on her knees in her oratory, frantically praying to the Lord of Hosts . . .

The first news was good: Sir Thomas Kyriel had

retaken Valogne. From there he marched along the coast with the object of joining up with Somerset, who had fallen back on lower Normandy. The Count of Clermont marched in pursuit of him, and Richemont, the Constable, lay across his route. On 15 April 1450 the three armies met at Formigny. Caught between two fires, the English fought savagely; but they were crushed, 4,000 of them were killed. Forgotten in Europe, thereafter, was the fame of Crécy, Poitiers and Agincourt, and English dominion in Europe. England was down; and would need two and a half centuries to rise again.

When Suffolk received the black news, he stoically prepared for death. He wrote his son a letter which was in some sort a testament full of religious faith and dignity, of a quality which proves that despite the greed and violence of the men of his class, the Duke had a high spirit and a noble soul. Having done which, he called his servants and people together and in their presence swore upon the Host that he would die innocent of the charges against him. Then, having freighted two small ships, he set sail for France with the intention of getting himself killed in battle.

But he had too many enemies set on making a quick end of him. He had not been long at sea when he met with the *Nicholas of the Tower*, one of the principal ships of the Royal Navy: and she was under Somerset's orders. Holding Suffolk's ships under the threat of her guns, her captain ordered the Duke to come aboard him. And as he set foot on her deck he was greeted by the captain with a curt, 'Welcome, traitor'.

The English have a taste for keeping to forms even when it comes to murder. The *Nicholas of the Tower's* officers and sailors formed a court and Suffolk was brought before it for trial. It was a clownish parody. The sailors were drunk, but less on wine than on the idea of having in their calloused hands one of the great Lords whose arrogance crushed them under foot. He would pay dearly now for his coat of arms, his silken garments and his castles, and the kisses of a royal mistress. A peer of England would find out what it meant to fall into the hands of a crew of poor, maltreated lads broken by the hardest work. They flung in his face all the charges which for months had been rumoured against him: conspiring with the enemy, plotting against his own country. And had he not proved his guilt by fleeing from the King's mercy to offer his sword to the French King? Impassive and haughty, Suffolk refused to utter a word. It was decided to put him to death on the following day at dawn. As a special mercy due to his rank, he was not to be hanged but beheaded.

The condemned man spent the night in a cable-locker, with irons on his legs. What bitter thoughts must have tormented him during that vigil. He had longed for wealth and power and extraordinary honours, and fate had granted them with remarkable speed, giving him dominion, titles, lands, the highest offices in the State, and best of all, the heart of the loveliest princess in Europe. All this within six years, only to end in this foul cell stinking of bilges. How beautiful Margaret had been that spring morning at Saint Martin-les-Tours. Why had he been so ardently bent on pleasing her? Why had he won her trust so quickly? But for her he would never have come to the governance of England, that implacable mistress who can forgive everything excepting the ineptitude of being unlucky.

At the first glimmer of dawn on 1 May 1450, he laid his head on the improvised block. A clumsy executioner, the sailor appointed headsman required six strokes of a rusty sword to separate body and soul.

It was from the Duchess of Suffolk, hastening to demand justice, that Margaret heard of her friend's death. Her grief was fearful. In this passionate, despotic woman accustomed to being all-powerful, despair at failing to save the man she loved came very close to madness. For three days the Queen refused all food and filled the palace with the sound of her weeping. Yet such was now the spirit of this nineteen-year-old girl that the news of a revolt raised in Kent by the Duke of York's agents at once restored her self-control. She had a double task to accomplish now: to avenge her dead, and save her husband from a like fate.

Out of this crisis the Queen emerged transformed. It was as if the rusty cutlass used by Suffolk's murderers had killed all pity in her, all fear and remorse, every weakness and every generous illusion. It had killed her youth. What remained was an amazon whose Spanish tenacity and Lorraine obstinacy combined were ready to face up to the assaults of a whole nation in a frenzy of rage.

# BOOK TWO

# The Tempest

# Jack Cade

Ever since his adolescence as a prince in disgrace and scarcely recognized, Richard of York had dreamed of power. All the obstacles between himself and the crown could not make him forget for a moment that he was the rightful heir. Yet his rival's seat on the throne seemed all too firm: half a century of unquestioned possession; Henry V's victories; the whole nation's, together with his own oath of loyalty; and the King's saintliness, these ensured it.

For a long time Richard had virtually given up all idea of attacking so strong a position. His hopes revived only when the unexpected course of events had shaken the very foundations of Lancastrian power.

Deprived of his uncles and of his most energetic minister, Henry VI seemed disarmed, almost helpless. The Duke took no account of the Queen, thinking her too young to be dangerous; nor of the discredited Somerset. The only serious obstacle now seemed to him to be the people's attachment to the victor of Agincourt's family. Before taking any direct steps he needed to know what were the real feelings of the mass of the people, and at the same time to remind them of his long-buried claim. His Irish exile enabled him to discover the means needed to stage a play with a message which would surely strike home to England's mind.

Jack Cade was not, as some have thought, a common mercenary soldier who happened to be uncommonly bold; nor was he a mere adventurer greedy for blood and rapine. Young, personable, lively, a gambler; a facile and ready talker, he enjoyed inviting fate to do her best or worst with him. A bastard without home or family, an artisan turned soldier, he had, for a while, fought in the French wars. Newly returned he had not settled to any course of life, when Richard of York set glittering before his eyes a ready-made play whose extravagance greatly attracted him.

And thus, one fine morning in 1450, an astounded England heard that the pretender Edmund Mortimer, supposed to have been dead for twenty-five years, was apparently very much alive.

This Mortimer was a direct descendant, through his grand-mother Philippa Plantagenet, of Lionel, Duke of Clarence, Edward III's second son. He had died very young, leaving as heiress his sister Anne, Richard of York's own mother. To bring him to life again was a clever way of drawing the people's attention to the claim of a prince whose throne had been usurped by the Lancasters—a claim which now devolved upon the House of York.

The movement did not, as might be supposed, begin in Ireland. There was, not far from London, a territory far more propitious for an undertaking of that kind: the county of Kent. A clever leader could easily talk one or other section of the populace into rebellion. Cade was such a leader. In an absurd but well-aimed proclamation he declared that the hated Frenchwoman, the Queen, was going to avenge her lover, Suffolk, on the poor peasants, to raze their houses to the ground and transform their country into a desert. The time had come to snatch King and Realm out of the termagant's hands. He, Mortimer, grandson of Edward III, would march on London, drive the money-changers out of the temple and, in accord with his nephew of York, set up a government of men who were at least honest. Nobody could have taken seriously the mischief-maker's claims touching his birth, it was very well known that the real Mortimer had been dead and buried for more than two decades; and had he been alive he would have been a middle-aged man, a great deal older than Cade.

That did not prevent a considerable body of men from rallying round the impostor: there were peasants and artisans convinced by his oratory, or quite simply greedy for loot, fishers in troubled waters hoping to turn the affair to some account, malcontents who really believed that England's fortunes could be restored by a *coup d'état*, and all the crop of ruffians and rascals who spring up at the first sign of civil disorder, like mushrooms after a storm. Cade collected 20,000 men and with this improvised army he marched on London, flanked by heralds of the Dukes of Exeter and Norfolk, keeping an eye on him for their masters, both trusty allies of Richard of York.

The news of this march on London found the court still stunned by the disasters in Normandy and by Suffolk's murder. The Council was now dominated by Cardinal Kemp and that venerable prelate, all wisdom and virtue, shrank from violent solutions. He was apt to encourage the King—sometimes to a dangerous extent—in his tendency to excessive indulgence and compromise. Margaret, indeed, had one or two more resolute men in her own circle—Lord Say, Lord Scales, Owen Tudor, and Sir John Fortescue, Henry's former preceptor. But she had not yet recovered her balance. She was hag-ridden by the fear lest her husband suffer the same fate as Suffolk, and in that state her mind swung between first one resolve then another contradictory one.

Meanwhile, Cade's army was gathering strength at every village he marched through. Drunk on the suddenness of his success and by the cheers of the populace, the adventurer was beginning to wonder whether he was not, in fact, Lord Mortimer. He played at dispensing justice and, to mark his comtempt for the laws, cut down royal oaks on his line of march.

Despite his horror of civil war, Henry at last made up his mind to raise an army. But who should command it? It might make its general into a dictator more dangerous than Cade himself. Margaret's choice was the two Stafford brothers, fourth rate soldiers perhaps, but utterly devoted to the Lancastrian cause and too simple minded ever to become dangerous rebels. The King was persuaded to march with his troops; his presence would be worth more than cannon. And Margaret, refusing to remain behind alone, at the mercy of nightmares of anxiety, insisted on sharing her husband's danger.

When the pseudo-Mortimer learned of the approach of a royal army, his nerve abandoned him. He had enough military experience to foresee the results of a clash between the pikes of several companies of old soldiers, and his own half-naked crew armed with pitchforks and mattocks. He therefore ordered a retreat which immediately became chaotic. Stafford's cavalry turned it into a rout and the rebellion was wiped out in two hours.

But the idea of spilling his subjects' blood was already tormenting the pious Henry with remorse. It did not occur to his generals to urge on him the clear necessity for following up their easy success with some decisive action. As for the Queen, torn by anxiety, in a hurry to remove the King from the hazards of a possible clash with the rebels, she could think of nothing but getting away from the camp. Her opinion prevailed and Henry returned with her to London. That was the sole occasion on which Margaret was wanting in resolution and showed ordinary feminine timidity.

Cade meanwhile had made use of the time to reorganize his forces, and the Staffords decided to disperse them again. They marched, but without knowing exactly where Cade was. However, they came up with him at Sevenoaks and this time the rebels could not avoid a fight. The terrain was difficult—so much so that it was quite unsuitable for the formal manoeuvres proper to a professional army at that time, and this was the ruin of the regular troops. Hampered in its movements, unable either to deploy or to charge, the King's army was routed. The Stafford brothers had no wish to survive defeat and fought on until both were killed. Cade stripped Sir Humphrey Stafford of his damascened armour by way of a trophy, and himself wore it with strutting arrogance. The country was stunned, but not really indignant; the fact was that a great many people were looking to 'Mortimer' to introduce those 'reforms'—nobody quite knew what reforms—which the whole Kingdom wanted.

Having confidence in his eloquence, Cardinal Kemp went to Cade's camp escorted by a prince of the blood, the Duke of Buckingham. The high rank of these plenipotentiaries succeeded in turning Cade's head completely. He assumed an arrogance worthy of Caesar after the conquest of Gaul: no, he would not go alone to London to present his demands to the King, as the Cardinal invited him to do. Let the King come to him, there in his camp. The King's person would be treated as sacred, but Cade demanded the punishment of his councillors and above all, the head of Lord Say. The Cardinal was forced to withdraw, having accomplished nothing.

At court there was a panic. Entrusting the defence of London to Lord Scales and Sir Matthew Gough, the King and Queen sought refuge at Kenilworth Castle in the north. Margaret wanted to take Lord Say with them, but the Treasurer nobly refused, for he was unwilling to compromise them by his unpopularity.

With Jack Cade in Southwark, demanding that the gates of the city be opened to him, the city Aldermen met, the Lord Mayor presiding, and with only one dissenting voice decided to open the gates. Lord Scales could do nothing but shut himself up in the Tower with Lord Say. Cade made a solemn entry into London: as he crossed the bridge he broke the chain with a blow of his sword, declaring, 'Now Mortimer is Lord of the city'.

He soothed the nervous fears of the burgesses, and forbade looting on pain of the severest penalties. He then besieged the Tower and forced Lord Scales to surrender the Treasurer, Lord Say. Anxious to respect legal forms, he would not order a summary execution. He summoned the terrified City Aldermen, forced them to constitute a court of justice, and to condemn the unfortunate man— guilty of having been Lord Suffolk's friend and the Queen's favourite, to death. It seemed that the impostor was now triumphant: he had won over the common people by making the rich financiers suffer the first rigours of his rule; and, with the same blow, compromised the city magistrates. The ordinary burgesses watched his progress with indulgence.

But not for long: only for as long as Cade's Kentish rabble could resist the temptation of the richly stocked London shops. As soon as looting started, the burgesses ceased their smiling and shrugging. Closing their shutters they seized the weapons which every good tradesman kept in the back of the shop. Street fighting broke out and Cade's peasants proved no match for the citizens, and soon found themselves flung back into Southwark, facing closed gates and raised drawbridges. Furious at this mortifying setback, they turned on their leader, and there was discord in the rebel camp.

The wily Cardinal Kemp at once seized his chance. As soon as he had news that the rebels were hesitating, looking sourly on their leader, short of victuals and discouraged by the heat, he crossed the Thames in a wherry, with Wayn-flete, the new Bishop of Winchester, to their camp. Armed with the Royal Seal, the two prelates promised an amnesty to all who would make immediate submission. In forty-eight hours the army was disbanded and the peasants, provided with a pardon bearing the seal of England, made smartly for their homes.

Only the pseudo-Mortimer and his principal lieutenants were excluded from the general pardon. They fled, taking their booty with them, but violent quarrels over the sharing of the spoils soon turned them against each other. Jack Cade therefore decided to seek his salvation alone. The government offered a reward of a thousand marks for the body of the rebel leader alive or dead. The greed which this stimulated made him a hunted man. After crossing the Medway by boat, he was recognized, surrounded and at last struck down by the Sheriff of Kent. The whole of this extraordinary adventure, which clearly demonstrated the progress of anarchy and breakdown in the realm, had run its course in two months.

But it had taught Richard of York what he wanted to know: the road of his ambition lay open before him.

On 10 July 1450 the King and Queen returned to London. Hardly had they begun to give thanks to Heaven when couriers from France brought news of fresh calamities.

# Somerset

After the surrender of Rouen, Somerset had fallen back on
Caen with an army that was still numerous, and his
artillery train still intact, so that he was in a position to
cover the whole of lower Normandy. Caen, one of the
most ancient and opulent towns of the Duchy, then held
rank as a royal city. During his Regency of France, Richard
of York had had it made an apanage of his own; and the
captain commanding its garrison, who naturally detested
Somerset, prided himself on defending the town in the
name of the Duke of York, his master.

Having rid himself of Sir Thomas Kyriel, Charles VII
mustered all his strength against this last of the English
territories. Very soon, Jean Bureau's cannon were thunder-
ing their balls into the town. The Duchess of Somerset was
there; and as she had proved in Rouen, she had, unlike so
many ladies of her day, not the slightest inclination to rise
above the natural weaknesses of her sex. This time her
courage was of even poorer temper: a stone, struck by a
cannon ball and falling between her and her children, the
poor wretch, frightened out of her wits, fell on her knees
before her husband and implored him to spare the lives
of his sons by capitulating. Trapped between a captain
contemptuous of his orders, a population yearning to be

restored to its old French obedience, and the crushing superiority of the French army, Somerset was beginning to lose his nerve. Under these circumstances he could not find the courage to deny his wife's tears yet another victory over his honour; he ordered the captain of the garrison to surrender.

He, however, being a man of very different mettle, flatly and categorically refused, declaring that he would force the Duke to be a hero whether he liked it or not. In a sullen rage, Somerset descended to treachery: he secretly urged the burgesses of Caen to throw open the gates to the French and they, all French at heart, took him at his word. Charles became master of Caen almost without striking a blow. As for Somerset, he seemed bent on positively wallowing in his cowardice: the price set upon his personal freedom was surrender of his artillery, England's last hope in France: he paid it.

Meanwhile the officer commanding Caen had managed to escape. He set sail, however, not for England but for Ireland where he went straight to the Duke of York with his news. Richard's annoyance at losing a valuable asset quickly gave way to joy at being offered the chance of a lifetime. His cronies, Norfolk, Exeter, Salisbury and above all his fiery nephew Warwick, persuaded him to seize it. They raised a force of 4,000 men and offered them to their leader. Richard made up his mind to cross his Rubicon. At the head of his little army he crossed over into England and marched on London with the declared intention of punishing the traitors.

But on that march he was forced to recognize that the country was not ready for a revolution. The people were cursing the Queen and her creatures at the tops of their voices, but the King's prestige was still intact, and Richard saw the reef he would be wrecked on if he went sailing ahead too fast. He therefore confined himself, when he reached London, to demanding justice for the wrong which

Somerset's cowardice had done him, while loudly protesting his loyalty.

Margaret was raging. What sort of a kingdom was this, where a serf could cut his sovereign's army to pieces, and the great officers of the Crown buckled on their armour and came sword in hand to make their complaints? She would have liked to receive York with a blast from the royal cannon. Alas, after the latest events the King had neither a soldier nor a penny piece. And Cardinal Kemp was again called upon to play mediator. He promised Richard that Parliament would be summoned as soon as possible and the Regent of France impeached.

Somerset, meanwhile arrived in haste to defend himself: he saw the Queen and pretended that he was concerned only to exculpate himself in her eyes. His danger made him clever, eloquent and plausible: why were they trying to strike at him? Because he was the only man of his rank left, capable of defending his master against seditious malcontents, and of raising a dyke against the Yorkist tide. What, above all, his enemies could never forgive him was his unshakable devotion to the Queen.

Margaret was at one of the most terrible crises of her life. At twenty years of age she was faced with the task of preventing, almost single-handed, the dismembering of an empire, and the collapse of a dynasty. There was not a man she could count on, barring a couple of aged priests; not a sword. For a woman as well as for the Queen, this tragic loneliness was more than she could bear. Last of the Lancasters, Somerset remained the only prince whose birth and interests made him a Royal champion. Forty-five years old, he was still able to please a woman, persuade, cajole and charm. Margaret was still in ignorance of his mysterious part in Suffolk's murder; she rejected charges brought against the Regent the moment her enemies made use of them as banners in their own cause. She turned eagerly, as to a liberator, to this man of straw, as

12　Charles VII (*Musée de Versailles: Cliché du Service de Documentation Photographique des Musees Nationaux*)

13  Portrait of Agnes Sorel, mistress of Charles VII (*Loches, Private Collection: Photographie Bulloz*)

weak-minded as he was craven-hearted. With all her customary ardent impulsiveness she gave him her confidence, her esteem and even her heart.

Are we to believe her enemies when they say that the Duke of Somerset became her lover? We have no more proofs of it than of her supposed affair with Suffolk. Still, it is difficult deliberately to set aside an accusation which seems to account for the young woman's foolish conduct, and her astounding audacity in defying all England for her new Minister's sake.

Especially recalled by the King, Parliament met at Winchester and Somerset was impeached at the Bar. Not without good reason, the Regent accused the Members themselves as responsible for his defeats, reminded them of the warnings they had been given in the preceding year, and of their criminal obstruction. He was only blamed the more furiously for his defections. And from the outset, the debate went far beyond the Norman battlefields. Partisans of the White Rose were dominant in both Houses: they condemned Somerset to imprisonment. The King ratified the sentence and the Duke was sent, amid jeers, to the Tower of London. Satisfied with their initial victory, Richard of York disbanded his army, and Parliament, its task accomplished, declared the session over.

That was the moment Margaret had been waiting for. She had managed to call together York's principal adversaries and believed herself in a position to act decisively. Her action was virtually a *coup d'état*. The forces at her disposal would perhaps not have sufficed to impose her will on the King and Council; but the fact is that among those uneasy, vacillating or unwordly men, her will, a will of iron, alone sufficed. She got her way, had Somerset released from the Tower and, to the amazed indignation of the whole nation, appointed him Constable of England. The Constable was supreme commander of all the armed forces which, in the circumstances, made him absolute

I

master of the government. To raise to that office the man associated with the country's defeat, the most unpopular man in England, was not merely to defy public opinion, but to flout it on a grand scale.

Margaret openly and proudly came out on the side of the Red Rose. By so doing she deprived the King of his rôle as supreme arbiter—that is, of his principal safe-guard—and bound his fate to that of a particular party. Her intention, no doubt, was to confront the rebels with a clear assertion of the royal authority. She had had enough, much more than enough, of the constitutional meekness, the abdication of that authority, which, for a year, had been required of her. She was blinded by her need for revenge, and her natural temerity.

The country was bursting with anger, the Duke of York breathed fire and slaughter, but no man moved a finger. People were exhausted by the vicissitudes of that tempes-tuous year and a harsh winter completed the lowering of their spirits. Besides, Margaret's audacity seemed to have put heart into Somerset himself. The dazed and stunned malcontents put up no more than a token resistence. It almost looked as if the realm, so long adrift, had found a new pilot.

On 6 January 1451, a little while before the King and Queen of England were about to take their seats at table to celebrate the feast of Epiphany, the Steward of the Household respectfully announced that there would be no dinner to be served, the tradesmen supplying the royal household having refused to deliver any more provisions on credit.

As a philosopher submissive to the divine laws, Henry VI doubtless remembered, at that moment, his uncle Charles of France and the jibes with which the English had formerly insulted the pauper prince who could not even find the money for a pair of new shoes. Now, while England was sunk into one of the worst financial straits in all her history, Charles, with full coffers and an incomparable army which was actually paid regular wages instead of being required to live by looting, was, despite the winter, preparing to complete the conquest of his heritage. Master of Normandy, after the taking of Falaise and Cherbourg, he was turning his attention to Aquitaine.

For the English, Aquitaine was not, like their other overseas provinces, a possession to which they were attached only by pride and greed. Normandy, and the territories which constituted the Plantagenet family apanage—Anjou, Poitiers—lost in 1204, had, in the two centuries before they were reconquered by Henry V become completely French at heart. Aquitaine was different.

Guyenne, Gascony were an integral part of the great family of countries, and not the least dear. Not since the marriage of Eleanor of Aquitaine to Henry II had any armed foreigner dared to set foot in them. Bordeaux was a metropolis, which for a long time rivalled London in wealth and prestige, and many an English sovereign had held his court there. Richard II was born there; and the Black Prince had lived there as Prince of Aquitaine. The city held many hallowed memories for the English, and in turn was affectionately devoted to its masters. Commercial considerations contributed to the maintenance of this state of mind: the Gironde wine-growers could not hope for better customers for their wine than the English. Consequently feeling ran high throughout the realm when the news came of the new French offensive, and the fall of Bourg, Blaye, Saint-Emilion, Castillon and Libourne.

Margaret was wringing her hands. All her pride and courage were involved in her desire that Henry VI have a reign worthy of those of his predecessors, and that he should restore England's greatness without Yorkist help.

Believing that only she herself, and Somerset, were capable
of succeeding in this task, she devoted herself to it body
and soul, undertaking the heaviest tasks and forcing herself
to apply her mind even to the most tedious and troublesome. Still only twenty-one, she had little experience and
no diplomatic flair; but her spirit was so ardent, her convictions so powerful that, had she been sustained by even a
small measure of popularity, she might have forced the
hand of fate itself. The national hero, Lord Talbot,
thought so and believed in her. The fiery octogenarian
soldier, who in his countrymen's eyes embodied all the
virtues of chivalry and all England's hopes, made a
cult of the Queen, which was in itself an invaluable
support.

But Parliament worked better for the French cause, than
even the Bureau brothers' cannon. What could the King
do without a penny to his name? And he could not, in
any case, raise an army without running the risk of seeing
its officers too busy fighting each other to fight the
French.

So Charles VII went calmly on with his conquest. At
his approach the Bordelais tried a sortie, but the first
artillery salvo put them to flight. On 5 June they opened
negotiations. The French king was remarkably moderate
in his terms: he would confirm the city's privileges; he
refused a ransom; and agreed that the citizens be free to
opt for himself or England. On these conditions Bordeaux
promised to surrender and open its gates in eighteen days
time if no help arrived from the English.

On 23 June the town herald appeared on the walls.
Three times he called 'those of England' to rescue 'those
of Bordeaux'. None having answered, he opened the
gates to Charles of France.

Bayonne, its citizens taking pride in their honour,
resisted until 23 August. Three hundred years to the very
day after the divorce of Eleanor and Louis VII, Aquitaine

was restored to the kingdom of France. The dismal tolling of this disastrous news throughout England pealed like wedding bells in Yorkist hearts.

The men of the White Rose cried 'Treason!' at Queen and Constable: the feeling of loss is summed up in Holinshead's *Chronicle*; 'in Aquitaine alone the kingdom was losing three Archbishoprics, thirty-four bishoprics, fifteen counties, one hundred and five baronies, a thousand *capitaineries*'; that, plus the abandonment of Anjou, Maine and Normandy constituted the balance sheet of the Queen's government, the dowry which she had brought England. Such was the agitation that the Yorkists believed themselves already victorious. When Parliament assembled again a Member of the Commons demanded that Duke Richard be adopted as heir presumptive to the crown.

He was premature; a majority of Members might hate Somerset and want to bring Richard into power, but they did not yet dare to raise the dynastic question. The King was still loved by the people. The more tragic his trials, the more did Henry's virtues acquire a majesty to which even the Yorkists themselves were not insensitive. The suggestion made by the Duke's over-zealous friend raised a storm of indignation in the Commons. A warrant was issued against him and he was haled off to the Tower.

This incident should have made clear to Richard the danger of premature intervention. But his hatred of Somerset was driving him to extremes; moreover, like all leaders of revolutions, he was forced to follow where his troops led, notably his young lieutenant, Warwick.

At twenty-four Warwick was not yet the great Earl, the Kingmaker, leader of the nobility, the clergy and the mob. But what he would become quite soon was already apparent. Fired and consumed by turbulent ambitions, yet never allowing his natural impulsiveness to obscure his clarity of judgement, positive, despising the archaic rules of chivalry and worshipping only his own interests, he had a remarkable power to inspire his soldiers with enthusiasm by his *bravura* attitudes; and both great and humble by means of a nicely calculated generosity. Warwick wanted to bring matters to a head at once, wanted it with a fervour not unconnected with his animosity against the Queen. That animosity went beyond the limits of even passionate political opposition.

Utterly and fiercely devoted to her friends as she was, Margaret never missed a chance of striking at her adversaries—even supposed ones—with ferociously sarcastic witticisms. The prestige of her beauty doubtless made the wounds she inflicted unforgivably painful. There is no reason why we should not believe that at the origin of Warwick's terrible hostility lay a grievance of that kind.

Be that as it may, Richard of York yielded to his friends' persuasions. He assembled a little army and again marched on London in February 1452. The pretext was the same as before: the sovereign must be snatched away from the nefarious influences which surrounded him. The Queen and Somerset judged the time come to oppose force with force, but at that point they came up against the King's opinion.

For Henry, civil war and its train of horrors was the worst of nightmares. He could not make up his mind to war with his own subjects, his family, to spill blood in the service of his personal interests. To avert that catastrophe, no sacrifice seemed to him too great, not even abdication. But the armour of his heroic abnegation had one flaw: his love for his wife. Margaret took advantage of it. She brought the one irrestible argument into play: if the Yorkists triumphed, what would become of her, handed over to the blind hatred of the nation? And with heart torn and troubled mind Henry gave orders to assemble the troops who were faithful to him; he would fight, but only for his lady.

The whole court marched with the army. Not even the Bishops dared to remain behind in a London stripped of its garrison.

On learning that the Lancastrians were up in arms, the Duke of York changed his line of march. He went south round London to fix his camp at Blackheath in Kent where, at the first sign that fortune was smiling on him, a horde of adventurers would be sure to join him. The Constable took up a position between him and the city, the two armies being encamped at a distance of two leagues from each other. Richard's situation was not of the best. His force was smaller than Somerset's and the local population maintained a disquieting neutrality.

Made energetic by his desire for vengeance and by Margaret's influence, Somerset asked the King for permission to attack. But Henry would not allow the killing to begin until he had exhausted every possibility of coming to terms. And Cardinal Kemp, imbued with the same ideas, was urging a compromise. A herald was therefore sent to the Duke of York calling upon him to return to his duty. Richard answered haughtily that he had never strayed from it. He would readily throw himself on his sovereign's clemency and would seek, under his orders, to restore order in the realm. But on one condition: the traitor Somerset must be punished.

When the bishops had taken in the tone of this message, they contrived to speak with the King in Margaret's absence. There can be little doubt that in his heart of hearts the Cardinal considered the Duke of York more worthy than Somerset to steer the ship of state. Henry was in any case inclined as always to prefer the way which would lead to peace. He gave orders to arrest the Constable. With a swiftness which was combined with a thoroughly churchmanly mystification, the Cardinal put this order into execution. The captain of the guard required the astounded Somerset to surrender his sword, while the herald galloped as fast as his spurs could drive his horse to announce the news to Richard of York.

Never for a moment doubting the word of Henry the Saint, the Duke disbanded—or appeared to disband—the companies of his partisans. And having done so he set out for the royal camp convinced that power was already virtually in his hands. So far so good: the King was a sick man, before long a successor must be looked for. Who would dare dispute the claim of Edward III's most direct descendant?

Meanwhile, the Queen, cleverly isolated by the Cardinal's contrivance, knew nothing of these events. She was informed of them by Somerset himself, for the captain of the guard had not thought himself qualified to refuse the Duke the favour of speaking to the Queen. When she thus heard of the transactions which Henry had sanctioned, she was possessed by a devastating fury, for an act of cowardice was something she could never admit to be necessary. In a blinding rage she rushed to her husband's tent, followed a few moments later by Richard of York himself.

The Duke began by protesting his loyalty: his sole concern and object was the country's well-being, and to that end only had he demanded that a felon be stripped of his office. At the word 'felon', one of the tent flaps was thrust suddenly aside, to reveal the Constable to the astonished eyes of the rest. Margaret had been foolish enough to allow him to hear what happened, on receiving his promise to remain hidden. There was an exchange of high-flown abuse between the two dukes until Richard turned to the King and said, 'I see that I have been deceived. I had too much faith in your word.' He left the tent, but Somerset had had time to place his own men, the Duke was seized and brought back to the King's tent. He declared that he had obviously been deliberately trapped.

No accusation could have wounded Henry more deeply:

knightliness was one of his ideals. But the current which was sweeping him away was too much for him, and his principles dated from another age. Trap, trickery and lies had become indispensable weapons, and in persuading her husband not to let his enemy escape the Queen was giving him good practical advice. York in the King's shoes would not have missed such a chance. But unfortunately, though the King and the Bishops occasionally resigned themselves to adopting an energetic policy, they never had the nerve required to persevere in it.

Inside twenty months, Richard had raised three insurrections; his arrest and summary judgement were clearly fully justified. And it would have spared England thirty years of violence and bloodshed. But the King, always ready to forgive, did not accept Margaret's view of the case. The Duke was taken to London and there was allowed to compound with a solemn oath, taken on the Host, never again to take arms against his lord; at which price he was allowed to go in peace to his own estate and there chew over his disappointment.

The Red Rose scored. The King seemed stronger than had been supposed, and several great families who had been sitting on the fence rallied to the Lancastrian cause. And for this some credit must be attributed to Margaret. For although her boldness and her tenacity, by now generally recognized, often provoked anger, they were also capable of arousing fanatical admiration. Margaret's beauty was now approaching its zenith; it no longer contained any element of simpering adolescent prettiness. Grave, poised, moving, it made as deep an impression on the heart of an octogenarian hero like Talbot, or a man 'of learning and good council' like Henry VI's tutor, Fortescue, as on the hearts of the lusty young cavaliers in her entourage.

The royal household led a life which should have won it

the respect even of its strongest adversaries. Henry divided his time between study and prayer. Margaret grudged not a single moment of her time to public business. What leisure she had was given to Queen's College or to the tapestry which she worked at with her ladies of whom the dearest, and likewise the loveliest, was Elizabeth Woodville, quite recently married to Lord Grey by the Queen's contrivance. Would not England now, at last, do her Queen justice? Margaret tried to push her advantage, to compel that popularity which still eluded her and which was becoming indispensible to the maintenance of the dynasty.

There were circumstances in her favour: Aquitaine was groaning under the light yoke of the French; Bordeaux, resentful at having to maintain a garrison, was watching its trade wither away, while vats of unsold wines piled up in the docks. If an English ship so much as showed her colours above the horizon, the citizens flocked to the harbour to welcome her company. Margaret seized this chance of recovering some territory. Her strong affection for her own family had probably undergone no change and her dearest ambition was to see an end to this eternal warfare. But Charles VII would no longer take part in any kind of negotiations and daily declared his determination not to lay down his arms until the whole of France had been reconquered; which caused the Queen deep distress. And the man who was urging this intransigent policy on Charles, the principal author of England's defeats, was one whom she found it impossible to hate, Pierre de Brézé.

The Queen conceived a simple and logical plan: she would, by means of a brilliant military success, at one blow reduce the distrust and hostility of her own subjects, administer a shock to French obstinacy, restore Guyenne to Henry and by means of that victory, impose a lasting peace on both belligerents. For the accomplishment of this purpose she had the cadre of a good army, and the most zealous and resolute of generals in Lord Talbot. But the continuing financial crisis, and the hostility of Parliament made her hopes illusory. Any other woman would have given up in despair, but Margaret persevered, using any and every means she could contrive.

In the first place, all Europe and notably the Duke of Burgundy were beginning to resent Charles VII's growing power. For some years a hidden struggle, a sort of cold war, had been going on between the French King and the Grand Duke of the West. Philip the Good was methodically laying a kind of siege to the Kingdom by a successful policy of acquisitions, alliances and conquests; and within the Kingdom he did his best to create disorder, by encouraging the Dauphin Louis' rebellions and uniting the great feudatories against the Crown. To this end he had himself paid the ransom of his old enemy, the Duke of Orleans, who had been a prisoner of the English since Agincourt; and he was even thinking of making advances to the house of Anjou.

But in 1452, one after another, his projects failed. The 'strangenesses and subtleties' of the Dauphin, relegated to his own Dauphiné, came to no more than his wedding the Duke of Savoy's daughter against his father's wishes. The opposition of the grandees evaporated in nothing more substantial than wordy complaints. Charles VII had had the financial genius Jacques Coeur, to whom he owed so much, arrested for lending money to the faction leaders; and he had asked Rome to rehabilitate the Maid, thus striking at both England and Burgundy. Finally, civil war was about to break out indeed, not in France however, but in the Duke's Flemish territories.

After having added new and tragic chapters to the centuries long tale of strife between the ancient communes and their lord, the city of Ghent had just broken down its bridges and tolled the great and terrible tocsin bell *Roland*, which called all men between the ages of eighteen and sixty to arms. The King of France had numerous ties and

139

contacts with the turbulent Flemish communes, which enabled him to check his dangerous neighbour's ambitious course. Victorious everywhere and having driven out the invader, should he now act, as many invited or urged him to do, in favour of the citizens of Ghent? Such action might initiate the collapse of the whole Burgundian empire.

In this extremity Philip remembered his old allies, the English. The Duchess of Burgundy, Isabel of Portugal, was a Lancaster on her mother's side. She was an energetic, crafty woman, experienced in public business which she often directed personally in difficult times. In Flanders in 1444 she had pacified the rebels in a dangerous rising and saved the Duke's lieutenant from them when they were trying to kill him. Isabel now approached her English cousins. Margaret must have had scruples about allying herself with the authors of all her parents' worst misfortunes; but the Duke of Burgundy was the richest prince in Christendom, and in matters of business there are occasions when personal feelings have to be ignored.

At all events, the King of England's purse was suddenly filled, and an army and a fleet were mobilized. On 21 October, Lord Talbot landed at Soulac in Guyenne. Bordeaux rose, imprisoned the French governor Coëtivy, and opened her gates to those she regarded as her countrymen. The Dauphin and the Duke of Savoy, against whom Charles had been about to act, raised their heads. And Ghent was left to face her liege lord alone. And it was with the utmost insolence that Philip received the ambassadors sent to make terms by the French king whom, a few weeks before, he had been humbly requesting not to help Ghent. As for the White Rose, it wilted sadly: a national success stilled even the most rebellious tongues.

Paying no regard to the inclement season, Talbot boldly continued his march and one after another walled towns fell to his arms. At the beginning of 1453, the Bordelais once again passed from French into English hands.

It looked as if Margaret's persistence had been rewarded. Fate itself seemed to be relenting at last, and turning to smile on her. At the end of February 1453 came more joyful news: the Queen was with child. Spreading swiftly across England this news rejoiced the hearts of all loyal subjects, and came as a terrible blow to the Yorkists. What weapons would be left to them against the mother of a Prince of Wales, who was also the architect of victory in France? As Margaret's star rose, Richard of York's declined.

# *The Battle of Castillon*

1453: end of the Hundred Years War; the Turks enter Constantinople; Flemish freedom is ended. 1453—it was one of the great milestones of history—seemed to be beginning well for Margaret, but bad news was on the way for her, as well as for others: on 28 November, her mother Isabel of Lorraine died in her forty-third year, worn out by heroic labours in two senses of the word—childbirths, and the work which should have been her husband's.

René mourned her noisily; then hastily sought consolation in the arms of a schoolgirl—she was hardly more—pretty little Jeanne de Laval whom he crowned without waste of time. Margaret had always been deeply attached to her family, excepting her sister Yolande (this attachment, by the way, was one of the chief complaints made against her); and bitterly she wept for the loss of a mother with whom she had spent but a few years of her short life, but whose life was her example. Especially at this moment, for never had Margaret been more keenly aware of the need for the harsher virtues, the only legacy which the dead woman had left her daughter.

For her uncle Charles was planning his revenge—albeit slowly, owing to the difficulties he was having with the grandees of his realm. And Talbot, anxious to take advantage of that respite, was nagging the Queen and the Constable for reinforcements. But the Yorkists were far from resigned to seeing 'the foreign woman' wearing the laurel crown, and Parliament was prevaricating and being thoroughly shifty.

Somerset was deplorably short of glamour and prestige. Margaret needed, at this juncture, to display quite exceptional energy. But this was the very moment—a decisive moment—when she was not only physically weakened by her pregnancy, but seriously disturbed by the King's condition.

The young sovereign was behaving more strangely every day, while Margaret, appalled, was doing her best not to recognize the symptoms of the disease that had afflicted his mad grandfather, Charles VI. Henry's nervous, peevish state grew daily worse; the slightest vexation upset all his faculties. Then he would fall into a strange lethargy in which his intelligence seemed extinguished. And worthy folk, seeing him so pale and almost insubstantial, had no doubt that their saintly monarch was in touch with the Unknowable.

But Margaret, who was less than normally sensitive to the superstitions of her age, was keenly aware of the danger. Treating her husband as an invalid, she did all she could to shield him from cares, or any kind of emotional disturbance, guarding him watchfully, and taking all the burden of government upon herself. But, unwell herself, and anxious, she was unable to overcome the obstruction raised by Parliament.

Summer came; and instead of the reinforcements Talbot had asked for, Guyenne was invaded by Charles VII's army provided with a formidable artillery train. To secure the Dordogne valley it laid siege to Castillon. Talbot marched to rescue the town.

The aged general does not seem to have been short of troops, as some have claimed. He had 8,000 men, a force equal to that which had been at the disposal of the Black Prince when, also operating from Bordeaux, he had annihilated King John's chivalry. But the recollection of their old disasters had quite cured the French of trying dashing offensives. Counting solely on trenches and cannon—the new weapons which the enemy had taught them the use of, they waited for Talbot behind their palisades.

*Quos vult perdere Jupiter dementat* . . . The English at Castillon showed themselves as blindly presumptuous as the French had done at Crécy. When the French, in an obvious feint, pretended a retreat by withdrawing a few companies from the front line, an officer ran to tell Talbot that the French were running away. The old soldier drew himself up and replied magnificently:

'Never will I hear a mass again, if I do not this day cut down these Frenchmen!'

And when an officer advised prudence, Talbot struck him across the face.

He led the cavalry charge against the French camp, his unfurled standard borne before him, a red velvet surcoat over his armour, so that he was a conspicuous mark for the enemy. But the time for such swaggering feats of arms was gone. Behind a palisade of sharpened stakes, Bureau's cannon were waiting: they fired a salvo all together, mowing down whole ranks of the English. Talbot nevertheless pressed on to the palisades, and there placed his standard. A second salvo killed both him and his son, after which English and French stood and fought over his body like the heroes of the Iliad over the body of Patrocles. Despite its heroism the English army was cut to pieces. Not until the following day, 17 July 1453, was Talbot's body found, so disfigured that it could be identified only by an old wound which his squire recognized.

Joan's work was completed, the English for ever '*bouté*

14 Troops disembarking in France; *Life and Acts of Richard Beauchamp, earl of Warwick*, by John Rous, c. 1485 (*London, British Museum Cotton Ms Julius E IV Art VI, fo. 25*)

15  Tomb of Pierre de Brézé and his wife (*Paris, Bibliothèque Nationale, Cabinet des Estampes, Collection Gaignières*)

16  Portrait of Edward IV (*Windsor Castle; reproduced by Gracious Permission of Her Majesty the Queen: A. C. Cooper*)

17 The Neville family at prayer (Paris, *Bibliothèque Nationale, Cabinet des Estampes*)

18 Portrait of John sixth Lord Talbot, Compton Wynyates, Tysoe (*Edwin Smith*)

*hors de France'*. But the French victory came too late to save Ghent; its citizen army was smashed on 23 July 1453 by Philip the Good at the battle of Gavre.

The terrible news caused a consternation so general in England that it seemed, for a brief while, to offer a chance of uniting the nation. Summoned by Margaret, Parliament assembled in haste. It was impossible to remain unmoved by the King's adjurations as, with tears in his eyes, he seemed to suffer in his own person from his country's terrible wound. In a unanimous impulse a vote to raise 20,000 archers—the size of Henry V's army of conquest— was carried. It was hoped by this means to save Bordeaux, already besieged by land and sea—a Bordeaux obstinately determined to remain English. But no sooner did the moment for acting on the vote arrive than private quarrels broke out again, and financial difficulties arose. It was resolved to cut the figure of 20,000 men to only 13,000. In the end, not a single soldier was enlisted.

The Queen wanted to stay in London where she could stoke the fire of patriotism which had been kindled in Parliament. But since the battle of Castillon Henry's health had gone from bad to worse. Margaret took him to Windsor, hoping that quiet and country air would help. But the invalid remained sunk in melancholy. On 15 August 1453, after eating a large meal of spiced meats, he became very sleepy. He slept, and when he awoke his mind was gone. The King of England was nothing but a shadow now—speechless, his memory and intelligence quite gone, a sort of sleep-walker incapable of uttering a word, or even expressing a wish or a want.

Juridicially, this catastrophe constituted an unprecedented ordeal for the kingdom. At that epoch the State existed only in the King's person and there was hardly a provision for such an eventuality as the sovereign's physical or mental breakdown. Thus England fell into the same lethargy as her prince. The omnipotence of Form, the very motor of her great political machine, made compromise of any kind almost impossible. Would not the Yorkists demand a deposition, or perhaps inspire some hot-head to commit a crime designed to release the land from this spell and reanimate the English spirit?

Cardinal Kemp and a few devoted friends of the House of Lancaster contrived to maintain a façade behind which the crude and barbarous learning of the physicians could do its best. Exorcism was tried, and aspersions with holy water; cauterism, bleeding, haemorrhoidals, purges—the patient was spared nothing. But at least Henry was able to avoid the torture to which his grandfather Charles VI had had to submit when men of science had tried to drive the devil out of him.

Summer passed without any change in the King's condition, and Margaret experienced the ultimate depths of mental and moral anguish. Few fates can be more poignant than that of this young woman isolated among a people with whom she was incompatible; stalked by so many enemies; in charge of a government undermined by defeat and anarchy; watching her husband sink into madness, and guessing what battles she would have to fight for the life of the child still in her womb?

Such perils would have broken any ordinary spirit: Margaret's emerged from the ordeal with new strength. Accepting the challenge of her lot, she marched into battle alone against all, braced by the fierce heroism she was to show to the very end.

By way of defiance to her enemies she decided to bear her child in London. On 13 October 1453 at Westminster Palace she gave birth to a son who was christened Edward and who bore the title Prince of Wales. There was yet another act of defiance in choosing Somerset as the boy's godfather.

Great was the rage of the Duke of York, henceforth obliged to choose between open revolt and renunciation of his claim to the throne. His partisans busied themselves spreading slanders all over the town: this prince who had been borne so opportunely bore no resemblance to the King; Somerset must be his father; or, stricken with barrenness, the accursed Frenchwoman had bought a child from a pauper woman and simulated pregnancy and confinement . . .

The fall of Bordeaux soon gave them a stronger case. That powerful city had maintained its resistance for two and a half months while trying to persuade Charles to renounce all reprisals. But the King was determined to make some examples. The story of the piece of play-acting which brought an end to resistance is well known: Jean Bureau sought out his master while the Bordelais delegates were with the King, and announced, 'Sire, I have found suitable emplacements for my batteries. If it please you, I shall have demolished the town in two days.'

Bordeaux yielded at that. The city had to pay an indemnity of a 100,000 crowns, and to build two citadels as guarantees of loyalty. Twenty citizens who had been particularly intransigent suffered confiscation of their goods and banishment. The Sire de Lesparre, who had handed the city over to the English, was executed. On 19 October Charles made his ceremonial entry: this time he had really reconquered his kingdom.

The White Rose soon scored another point: an ancient custom required that the King should have his heir recognized by presenting him in his arms to the assembled Peers. Until that formality had been gone through the legitimacy of the Prince of Wales could be called in question. Unfortunately, poor Henry's mind was sunk in a state of waking unconsciousness so total, that it seemed very difficult to get him to go through even this simple ceremony. A delegation of twelve lords spiritual and temporal went to Windsor where Margaret was keeping the sick man. Parliament was about to meet in order to lay down the law touching the infant prince's rights and the reorganization of the government. But nothing could be decided legally without the King's 'good pleasure'. All attempts to make Henry acknowledge his son failed.

Cynically, the White Rose exploited this situation. Was not the Queen's infamous conduct now glaringly apparent, since Henry the Saint refused to acknowledge the child of her adultery? The Earl of Warwick was the most determindly bitter of her detractors.

An assembly of Lords met together at the Nevilles' before the next session of Parliament. There Warwick spoke against the Queen with a fury which betrayed a secret personal feeling of the strongest kind: kitchen gossip, the slanders of jealous rivals, obscene tittle-tattle, degrading libels, nothing came amiss to him in filling out his indictment of the baby's right to bear the name of Lancaster. Never had so much foul mud been slung into the private boudoir of a Queen.

Nor had fate finished with her yet, not by any means. The next blow was the death of Cardinal Kemp. Although his influence had not always been used as the Queen would have wished, the prestige of his high ecclesiastical rank had been a sort of shield for the Lancastrian cause, and also it had helped to offset Somerset's unpopularity.

Parliament was reassembled. The delegation of twelve peers gave an account of their mission to Windsor. The Yorkists tried to raise the question of the prince's legitimacy; but by overstating their case, they ruined it, for Members were not prepared to follow them to such lengths. Consequently Prince Edward's title was confirmed without further debate, as likewise the apanage which went with it. This made it clear to Richard of York that he would achieve his ends only by seeming to serve the

King. Nobody would be deceived, of course, but English ways of doing things in proper form would be satisfied. The Duke accordingly asked to be made Protector of the realm, in order to safeguard the King's interests during his sickness. A royal order to that effect was assumed to have been given, and Richard was appointed Protector on 27 March 1454. He had thus taken the first step along the way of his ambition: he had the royal power; the sceptre and the crown were not so far out of reach.

Margaret was indignant, of course. On her own initiative she drew up a protestation, demanding from Parliament the Regency for herself. And no document in existence demonstrates more clearly the tragic divorce separating the Queen from her subjects: despite her 'learning' Margaret had never made a study of English institutions; but even had she done so she would not have been able to humble her pride and accept the implication of principles still unheard of in other kingdoms. Magna Carta, and the Provisions of Oxford, all those liberties which had been fought for during two centuries and were venerated in direct proportion to the strife and determination they had cost, were quite alien to her way of thinking. The arguments which she advanced in favour of her Regency would doubtless have impressed French lawyers with their strong preference for Roman Law; they were precisely those most likely to offend the touchy susceptibilities of Englishmen, jealous of their rights. With every phrase in which she invoked the law, she was unwittingly breaking it.

Richard of York's position was strengthened by this, and he was quick to take advantage of it. Arrested in the Queen's own apartments, Somerset was impeached at the Bar of Parliament, stripped of his office as Constable and thrown into the Tower. As for Margaret herself, relegated to Windsor with the King she was forced to lead the life of a recluse, almost a prisoner. Poor princess, whom the future had once seemed to smile upon so brightly! Now she had nothing, neither husband, nor friend, nor family, nor power. But she had her child; and for his sake she gathered her strength, ready to resume the struggle.

# The Wars of the Roses

Henry's mind had been wandering in regions unknown for fifteen months when it began at last to reanimate the poor gentleman's body. Upon learning that her husband had just, after so long, uttered a few words, Margaret almost fainted with the shock of hope restored. She at once gave orders for a Mass to be celebrated in the palace chapel and that prayers were to continue day and night continuously until the King's cure was complete.

She had several weeks still to wait before seeing the invalid recover his full awareness of the ordinary world, take marvelling notice of his newborn son, and, weeping, kiss his wife as if after a long and cruel absence. By early January 1455 the King's senses seemed to be completely restored.

Only a small number of his most loyal friends were aware of the miracle. As a good general, the Queen was counting on surprise to ensure that her plan against the Protector would succeed. Maybe, in other circumstances, she would have taken greater care of the King's health, which it must have seemed dangerous to expose quite so soon to the excitement of a *coup d'état*. But henceforth her chief concern was for her son; above all and at whatever cost, she must ensure an unshakable throne for the Prince of Wales.

One morning that winter, Henry VI, surrounded by a

numerous escort, appeared without warning before an astounded House of Lords. He did not announce *L'Etat c'est moi*! Nothing could have been more alien to his nature than such arrogance. On the contrary, he thanked his loyal Parliament for having taken such good care of the Kingdom during his illness. Now, Heaven be thanked, he could again take up the burden of government, lightening his servants of that heavy charge. With that, he withdrew the Protectorate from the Duke of York and dissolved Parliament.

His speech was greeted by the Lancastrians with enthusiastic cheers. The partisans of the White Rose looked at each other in silent consternation: against the King's will spoken with his own mouth, nothing could prevail. The Parliament must either submit or rebel. And no man yet felt ready for rebellion. The Members and Peers dispersed and Richard of York, outwitted once again, returned to his own castles. Somerset resumed office as Constable, passing from prison to power with an ease which seems curiously modern.

One man did not accept this *fait accompli*: Warwick. In the strife which now began the real leaders on each side emerged clearly; Margaret and the Earl.

Warwick shamed Richard for his submission: the right riposte to a surprise move was a surprise move; they should repeat, but under better auspices, the abortive attempts of 1450 and 1452. The Nevilles, the Beauchamps, the Norfolks and the Exeters were among the greatest landowners in the kingdom. Despite their exactions, despite the patriarchal customs still honoured, despite all these things, a common hatred of the central power still sustained between lords and vassals the full vigour of feudal solidarity. Petty lords and mere villeins alike hastened to rally to their overlords' standards, thus providing Richard of York with reliable troops, at whose head he at once marched on London.

The suddeness of this event took the Court aback. The Queen and Somerset had found matters in the most lamentable state, worse than they had ever been: York, during his Protectorate, far from overcoming the difficulties he had inherited, had created fresh ones. The common people were exasperated, the burgesses uneasy, the treasury completely empty, and the army almost non-existent. The King and Queen addressed a pathetic appeal, such that no loyal gentleman could ignore, to their nobles. But the Lancastrian lords were far from their lands, there was not time enough to call up their men, and raise a professional army.

In these circumstances there rallied to the King and Queen in their peril an army of knights in which even those holding no rank at all bore names among the oldest and noblest in the realm. An army? It was scarcely more than an escort, barely 2,000 men with whom Somerset was to try to stop an enemy six times as numerous.

The people of England watched this duel between the lords with apparent detachment and with mixed feelings. They liked the Duke of York, detested Somerset and regarded the Frenchwoman with obstinate antipathy. But Henry the Saint was still their idol; it seemed as if even his sickness had enhanced his prestige. There were good souls who affirmed that he had converse with God and the angels, and there was talk of sores healed by a touch of his hand, miracles wrought by his second sight. Alas, he was but a man, a poor wretch horribly wrought upon by the appalling legacies of his blood and the savagery of his nobles; pious, pacific and charitable, and thus a foreigner to his time.

Falling in with the Constable's wishes he marched with his loyal friends, while Margaret went to Greenwich, there to sit down and wait for news.

Too weak to confront the enemy, the Lancastrians entrenched themselves in St Albans in Hertfordshire; and very shortly the army of the White Rose encamped outside the town.

Despite Warwick's objurgations Richard of York hesitated to start a battle with his sovereign, and meanwhile Henry was insisting that a messenger be sent to the rebels under a flag of truce. This messenger brought back the Duke's usual ultimatum: Somerset must be dismissed. This time there were no ecclesiastical machinations and the herald returned to the Yorkists to declare that the King considered this demand an insult. Warwick, commanding the vanguard, was the first to hear this answer, whereupon, without awaiting orders from his chief, he himself ordered an attack. This then, was the manner in which the War of the Roses began, on 22 May 1455.

Warwick surrounded St Albans and soon forced his way into it. Ringed by enemy pikemen, the Lancastrian cavalry suffered a hail of those redoubtable arrows to which the English had owed their victories at Crécy and Agincourt. One of them wounded Henry VI in the neck and he was taken into a convenient bakers shop for a first aid dressing; and there he waited for the issue of the battle, shedding tears over the blood which was being shed.

That issue was not in doubt; overrun, the loyalist lords saw that the day was lost. But honour, at least, could still be saved and they hurled themselves against the encircling wall of pikes with all the heroism which sometimes makes us forget their faults and even their crimes. Their advantage was brief: Warwick counter-attacked furiously, and one by one they—Clifford, Stafford, Northumberland, the flower of the loyal nobility—were overwhelmed by the avalanche. Somerset fought on, fighting under his standard, as if he were seeking to redeem the manifold shame of his past. He fell at last, and the horses of the Yorkists trampled him under foot. Thus perished Edmund Beaufort, Duke of Somerset, Constable of England, whose cowardice had lost Normandy, caused Suffolk's murder, involved the Crown in civil war, and brought the Queen to the edge of the abyss.

The army of the Lancastrians having been annihilated, Richard of York rode into St Albans and there, on one knee before the King, cried, 'God be praised, Sire, the traitor Somerset is dead!' And that was the shock too many for a brain only just recovered from sickness. Once again Henry's mind withdrew from the horrors of this world. Reduced to the state of an automaton, the King let himself be carried to London like a captured banner.

Such was the first battle of St Albans; its importance lies less in the Yorkist victory than in the hecatomb of the Lancastrian lords. The savagery which was to mark the strife between the two factions and to become a by-word, has its origin in that slaughter. Every fallen lord had sons, vassals and friends who swore eternal hatred of the other side. The struggle between the two dynastic families from that moment assumed, even in the least of noble houses, all the bitterness of a personal quarrel.

In London Richard did not yet dare to push the consequences of his success too far. He summoned Parliament and demanded the reimposition of the arrangements which had been adopted during the King's illness, since Henry had again fallen into the same state of lethargy. At the beginning of July the Duke again received the Protectorate. Meanwhile he had forbidden the Queen to come to London, and furthermore, at Warwick's suggestion, he caused both Houses of Parliament to pass resolutions deploring the part which she had played and adding that her rule and Somerset's had been 'great tyranny'. Margaret was obliged to suffer these humiliations in silence. Venal interest, and their fear of what might happen to them, deprived her of her closest servants. But her request to be entrusted with the care of her husband was granted. Whereupon, a tireless Penelope, she began, in the shade of the trees of Greenwich Palace, to weave a new web.

Hardly were the reins of government in his hands when Richard ran into the difficulties entailed by a victory won by violence. The people expected him to work miracles which were quite beyond his power; then there was the greedy pack of his followers to satisfy and that entailed dissatisfying those great families which were not yet committed to either side.

Among those demanding favours, the Nevilles, father and son, were the most voracious. Warwick, then twenty-seven years old, got himself appointed Lord High Admiral and Governor of Calais, that is to say, absolute master of the Channel. He made the most of it by involving himself in a shady and very profitable contraband business, selling his protection to the pirates who swarmed in the Channel, and then posing as champion of the continental *bourgeoisie* by selling them, cheap, their own merchandise, intercepted on its way to them. This soon became very big business indeed, a sort of hijacking on a vast scale, comparable to the bootlegging which afflicted the United States during the Prohibition period. Not daring to protest, the merchants and traders resigned themselves to a state of affairs which gave them the illusion of robbing their competitors and ensured them a powerful patron at court.

Patron, indeed, Warwick was determined to be, and of clients innumerable; and he played the part with a magnificence without precedent. He kept open table for hundreds at every meal. Carefully fostered rumour spread the tale of his largesses, his helpfulness to any trader who was in difficulties, any freebooting captain threatened with retribution for some crime of violence, any younger son on the look out for a protector. His star was rising at a pace which was alarming, drawing into its orbit a universe of satellites. He used his power to nag and harass his uncle, urging radical measures which the Protector still shrank from.

Richard wanted and tried to avoid alarming anybody and to win the confidence of the Clergy. But above all he wanted to acquire a standing, a prestige which would place his authority beyond question. And that was a talisman he could find only in France. He opened negotiations. Charles VII's court was swarming with malcontents among whom the Duke of Alençon was one of the most restless. Alençon was a prince of the blood, a Valois, great-grandson of that brother of Philip VI who at Crécy had ordered the massacre of the Genoese archers forming the vanguard of the French army, because they got in the way of his charging knights. Formerly he had served his King well, notably when he rode at the Maid's side. But now he considered himself ill-rewarded, despite his enormous Normandy governorship. Like most of the great feudatories he was alarmed at the growth of the royal power, and was seeking to contrive an independent domain for himself.

To that end he did not hesitate to open negotiations with the national enemy. He promised that if York landed in France, he would deliver up to him all the fortified towns in Upper Normandy and a large amount of artillery —900 bombards at least, but he would try to do better and make it a 1,000. Richard was already making ready. A victorious campaign might put the crown on his head in a few days.

Margaret, meanwhile, having learnt a bitter lesson, had made up her mind to try no new move without being sure of lasting success. But she was secretly gathering about her a following of well-tried supporters, whom she was finding in those families which had lost a father or a son at the battle of St Albans: first, there were the Constable's two sons, the elder of whom was now the Duke of Somerset; then Owen Tudor and his sons, the Earls of Richmond and Pembroke respectively; Fortescue; the powerful Percy family; Lords Grey and Wiltshire; the young Clifford thirsting for vengeance; and numerous prelates steered by the Bishop of Winchester. A war chest was amassed in secrecy, and an army created without arousing suspicion. Exasperated by Yorkist excesses, public opinion was veering in favour of Lancaster. Now there was nothing to be done but wait for the King's mind to be restored to him again. That happened during the winter and at an eminently favourable moment. Too intoxicated by their success to heed the lessons of the past, the Yorkists were off their guard, the more so in that Richard did not believe in Margaret's strength. He thought that with Somerset out of the way, he had no dangerous enemy left in the royal camp.

Far more worrying was division in his own ranks. The problems of sharing the spoils of power were setting the victors against each other. To avoid brawls the Protector had even had to disperse his army; and now he had to leave London to settle a dispute between two of his lieutenants.

Margaret saw and seized her chance. On 24 February 1456 Henry went through the same performance as in the previous year. He appeared suddenly before Parliament, thanked his good (but absent) cousin, and withdrew the Protectorate from him; and as before, Parliament bowed to his wishes. And this time the White Rose could do nothing. Every strategic point round London was occupied by Lancastrian men-at-arms and the Yorkists moreover were at each others throats. Richard judged it wiser to wait for the luck to change. Trusting to the fact that nobody would dare to lay a finger on him, he withdrew to his own estates again; his partisans followed his example.

This setback to Richard of York was Alençon's ruin. The Duke was arrested on 27 May and brought to trial before his fellow Peers. Only the intervention of the Dukes of Brittany and Burgundy saved his head. At last fate seemed to smile on Margaret. The Yorkist government's faults gave the Lancastrians a measure of popularity. After her years of failure and humiliation, Margaret felt herself to be more surely the ruler of England than she had been since her arrival on the scene.

# *Reconciliation*

At twenty-six years of age Margaret of Anjou had wide experience in the wielding of political power. Yet her mind and spirit did not have the fine temper of a Catherine the Great's or an Elizabeth of England's. She had no talent for diplomacy, none of the diplomat's deep knowledge of the human heart, no duplicity, none of the necessary craftiness, and no control over her impulses.

To some extent she made up for these flaws by her force, her courage, her will, and the charm which radiated from her person. But she no longer made use of that charm for any but political ends. As we have said, her heart may have had its say once or twice during the first years of her marriage. But since the birth of the Prince of Wales all the powers of her affection were concentrated on the child and all her thoughts on safeguarding his heritage.

Young Somerset was nominally her chief minister, but the real work of that office was done by Waynflete, the Bishop of Winchester, who was appointed Lord Chancellor in 1456. To avoid disturbing the King and to preserve him from again being shocked into torpor, he was kept in isolation, following his usual occupations—reading, prayer, and hunting. In matters of public business he was only shown a report from time to time, and those only the

19   Harlech Castle, Wales (*Wim Swaan*)

20   Fifteenth-century battle scene (*Paris, Bibliothèque Nationale Ms. fr. 2691, fo. 38*)

21  Kenilworth Castle, Warwickshire from Grose's *Antiquities of England and Wales Vol. IV* (*London, British Museum: John R. Freeman*)

22  Chinon, France. A view from across the River Vienne showing (left to right) the Château du Coudray, and the Château du Millieu (*Wim Swaan*)

most cheerful; thanks to which poor Henry's health now seemed to grow stronger.

London had become so odious to the Queen that she had moved the court to Coventry Castle, which lay at the heart of the Lancaster country; there she knew herself to be safe from a surprise Yorkist attack; and there for several years she was able to reign as she had dreamed of doing. There, too, following her father's example, she surrounded herself with artists and scholars. Drawn by her beauty, the flower of the nobility composed her court, which became one of the most brilliant in Europe. The Queen protected those industries which we would call luxury trades, founded schools and hospitals, and entertained nobly. But she was to do more than that, to show herself in person to her people; that people to whom slanderers had for ten years been presenting a false idea of their Queen.

To that end she made a number of progresses with Henry and the young prince. Her grace, her gentle kindness, the sweetness of her manner when receiving, combined with the King's piety and the little boy's charm, won over many a partisan from the White Rose. Yet over all lay a deep uneasiness, caused by all those Lords, fiercely at watch and ward in their fortified castles, waiting their chance to fly to arms again.

In 1458 Margaret believed herself in a position to make an end of that. Her plan was clever enough, but revealed an excess of generosity which was perhaps due to the King's wishes, but also bears the mark of feminine idealism. Henry VI wrote a letter in his own hand asking the Duke of York to save England from civil war. He, the King, granted a full and complete pardon to those who had offended him. As for the private quarrels and law suits born of pernicious strife, he desired that they be settled as the outcome of a grand congress in which all the rival Houses would take part.

After some hesitation, the Lords agreed to this, some with genuinely peaceful intentions, others in order to avoid the obloquy of refusing. Nevertheless, they took their precautions; no nobleman risked his person in London without the escort of a considerable following. In some cases these retinues numbered more than 1,500 men. Moreover the burgesses, fearful of looting by these private armies, raised an army of their own. London took on the aspect of an embattled city, crowded with troops in particoloured liveries, snarling insults at each other in a score of local dialects.

In this warlike atmosphere the peace congress met at Westminster in the early part of 1458, presided over by the Archbishop of Canterbury. The arguments frequently became bitter and several times threatened to degenerate into a pitched battle. At last, after two months of diverse transactions, bargaining and exchange of promises, a formula for a general settlement was reached, and a national reconciliation accomplished. Then and only then did the King and Queen return to their 'good town' of London.

By way of solemn celebration of this unhoped-for event, and of giving thanks to Heaven, a sumptuous parade was organized. Wearing crown and ermine Henry led the Peers of the realm walking in pairs, to St Paul's Cathedral. As a symbol of the occasion each pair was composed of hitherto mortal enemies. The Queen walked in the procession with her hand in Richard of York's.

Thirteen years earlier in Rouen, Margaret had once before crossed the threshold of a cathedral with her hand resting on Richard's fist. How many tragedies those thirteen years had seen. Was it really possible to believe that they could safely be relegated to the past? Only one person there present, the King, had really forgiven all trespasses against him, and forgotten old injuries, in his passion for peace.

That peace was acclaimed with such fervent cheering along the route of the procession that for several months it was possible to believe that it had come to stay.

But, unfortunately, Warwick was only awaiting his chance.

Fearing to provoke him into wrecking the congress, the Queen had not dared to relieve him of his offices. But the Earl was well aware that she would do so at the first favourable opportunity. What, under a hostile government, would become of his profitable piracy and smuggling business? Let England perish, provided her ruins might serve as foundations for Neville greatness.

Warwick pirated and looted some ships belonging to the Hanseatic League. The Hanse towns protested energetically in London. Glad of a chance to avenge herself, the Queen summoned the Lord Admiral to explain himself before the Council. Warwick obeyed the summons, but escorted by his livery of 700 or 800 men wearing his scarlet surcoats, who followed their Earl into the very antechambers of the Palace, to the scandal of all worthy people. The Queen insisted that the Earl must stand trial. On the second day of the trial, an insurrection broke out, fomented chiefly by the always turbulent students. The mob murdered the Attorney General. The Queen used her pikemen to restore order, and flung masters and Aldermen pell-mell into prison.

The ensuing calm did not last long. During a sitting of the court trying Warwick, some of his men had slipped into the kitchens, on the prowl. A brawl developed between them and the royal cooks and scullions when one of the Yorkists referred to the Prince of Wales as a bastard. The fighting spread all over the palace and as Warwick came out of the Council chamber he was nearly stabbed by one of the scullions armed with a spit. He was forced to flee and take refuge on the other side of the Thames. From there he published to the four winds that the Frenchwoman had tried to murder him. Margaret riposted by giving orders to seize or kill him. Warwick escaped to Yorkshire, where he joined his father and his uncle and upbraided them for their flabbiness and inaction. Responding to Warwick's urging, Richard made up his mind to issue a proclamation in which he claimed the crown.

The Queen's response to this was to have a Bill of Attainder voted in 1459 by Parliament against the rebels; this amounted to proscription; thus denounced as outlaws, the Yorkists realized that they had only two alternatives: a victorious war against the Lancastrians; or life as hunted criminals ending in a shameful death.

The two parties confronting each other disposed of approximately equal forces. But the White Rose had one advantage in the quality of its leaders: there was first Richard's high standing, then Salisbury's military skill, and Warwick's audacity. They had, moreover, just discovered a new leader who at eighteen years of age was already showing remarkable talent as a soldier—Edward Plantagenet, Earl of March. To these resolute and experienced men, the Red Rose could oppose only Somerset's inexperience, the devoted courage of the Tudors, the wisdom of one or two prelates, and the savage energy of the Queen.

Anxious as always to make the right impression on the people, the Yorkists did not fail to put it about that the Frenchwoman was conspiring with Charles VII and asking for aid from the national enemy. And this time their allegations do not seem to have been mere slanders. Pierre de Brézé had been appointed Seneschal of Normandy with orders to 'observe' events in England. That bold warrior's attachment to the house of Anjou was well known to everyone, and some were ready to add that he was romantically attached to the Queen. It was even said that

Margaret got a number of her political and military inspirations from her former *chevalier servant*.

The English had a singular respect for Brézé because of the fear which he inspired in them. They held him to be the most redoubtable of all the French King's officers, especially since his raid on Sandwich in 1457, when he ravaged the port and countryside. Bourcier claims* that that expedition had been organized in accord with Margaret; but its date makes us reject this idea; for at that time the Queen had both factions under control and could have had no reason to call in the French; in fact to do so would have been contrary to her own interests.

But in 1459, deprived as she was of reliable advisers, did Margaret in fact turn, in her extremity, to the man whom, even after so many years, she remembered so well? We may suppose that she did do so, since it is a fact that Brézé's agent Doucereau accompanied the Red Rose armies and was present at their battles. There was no such thing as a war correspondent in those days and Doucereau's neglect to conceal his French connections makes it quite clear that he was not simply a spy. He was, incidentally, captured by the Yorkists at the battle of Northampton.

The strife very soon assumed the fratricidal virulence which was to characterize it thenceforward: only kinsmen can hate each other with quite such rage and ferocity. And kinsmen they all, in some sort, were: Warwick, grandson of a Beaufort, was twice cousin to Somerset, since his wife was a niece of the dowager duchess who was born a Beaufort. And since Edmund, Earl of Richmond, had married the daughter of another Beaufort, he was also connected by marriage with the Tudors.

Such common origins—and hence, sometimes, common interest—sharpened the appetite for killing. It is not possible to excuse these men by invoking the strength of

---

* In an article in the *Revue Historique d'Anjou*.

their convictions. Their two dominant—and apparently contradictory—characteristics—were fickleness and relentlessness. They were for ever changing sides, and fighting with equal fury first on one and then on the other.

Old England was plunging, with mad rage, a sort of demented joy, into an orgy of self-torture. Even in the best of them, in women and children as well as in the men, ordinary decent human feeling was swept away by this tidal wave of blood-thirsty madness. They became drunk on blood, and humanity was at last to be found only in the heart of the King who was thenceforth destined to be a sacrificial victim until his death.

Hostilities began with Salisbury's victory over a Lancastrian force at Blore Heath in October 1459. Margaret manged to recover the advantage, but when she returned to Coventry where she proposed to spend the winter, the young Earl of March took a force into London and the wildly excited Londoners handed their city over to the Yorkists.

Great efforts were made by both sides in preparation for the spring campaign. Margaret, at the head of a powerful army nominally commanded by poor King Henry, marched against the White Rose. The two armies clashed at Northampton on 9 July 1460. It was a great battle which the Queen, now accustomed to see bloodshed, watched from the top of a bell tower, accompanied by her son and a few guards. The Lancastrians at first had the advantage, but when one of their leaders and the companies he led defected to the enemy, his defection cut their army in two. They were defeated and driven from the field, and once again the King fell into rebel hands.

When she saw that the day was lost, Margaret's first thought was to save her son. She mounted her horse and fled, with the prince and their baggage and a dozen guards and servants. Unhappily, after riding a few leagues, they ran into a Free Company, that is to say one of the gangs of bandits and robbers which infested the countryside, and held fugitives of either side indifferently to ransom. The Queen had to buy them off with her money, her plate and her jewels. Deserted by her guards, she was wandering nearly desperate and quite lost, when by a miraculous chance she met with Owen Tudor and a handful of his men. It was from them that she heard that Henry had been captured.

The first consideration was to put the Prince of Wales in a safe place. This seven-year-old boy was now the one hope of the House of Lancaster and their followers. If the Yorkists got their hands on the child his life would not be worth a day's purchase. Owen Tudor was a Welshman and in his own still half-wild country he had loyal friends whose rule over their own lands was, thanks to their mountains, more or less sovereign. He therefore conveyed the Queen and her son to one of these friends, the castellan of Harlech Castle in the Cambrian mountains. Safe within those stout and rugged walls, Margaret waited, impatiently, for her chance to resume the struggle. Under the repeated blows of adversity her heart was hardening; and her spirit was closed to those feelings which had formerly made it beautiful. When her turn came her enemies would be able to look for no quarter, hope for no mercy.

Richard of York made a triumphal entry into London, like a Roman emperor, dragging the King in his train as if poor Henry had been a slave tied to the Duke's triumphal chariot. The common people yelled and cheered with joy.

But that joy was by no means shared by Parliament. As sometimes happens in many assemblies in which chicanery and obstruction reign, it was badly frightened upon realising that its goal had been all too thoroughly attained. Parliament had wanted to see the White Rose succeed, certainly; but to succeed within the bounds of legality.

Not a single member of the Commons was prepared to envisage those bounds being overstepped. As for the clergy, while they might, at a pinch, agree to the Duke of York's Protectorate, they would not even hear of a change of dynasty.

The two Houses meeting together awaited the victor of Northampton. Richard made his way to the palace, making his spurs ring as he crossed the floor to place one foot boldly on the lowest step of the empty throne. He hoped for a spontaneous burst of cheering, a vote by acclamation which would of itself proclaim him from that moment King of England. Peers and Members alike remained silent. At last the Archbishop of Canterbury plucked up courage and said,

'Will it please your lordship to go and greet the King?'

It was a sharp reminder that Henry and only Henry was still the Lord's Anointed. Richard flushed and answered,

'I know no man in this kingdom who should not first greet myself.'

And he left the hall in a rage.

Parliament could find no way out of this impasse. The Duke of York, persisting in calling himself the only legitimate heir to the throne, claimed the crown as of right. The blood of the Mortimers, three victories, and 20,000 men under arms, seemed to constitute irrefutable arguments in his favour. But there was no law which permitted the deposition of a King crowned and anointed in good form and according to the rites, and to whom the whole nation had sworn an oath of allegiance. After days of barren debate, the Peers and Members of Parliament ended by adopting a strange solution to their problem, a solution which still constitutes, down the centuries, the most moving tribute ever paid to a reigning monarch's conscience. A delegation was sent to Henry to beg him, himself, to decide on which side lay truth and right. And since this was a question which that saintly man had very often asked himself, he had his answer ready; he appealed to the right of custom, to his father's and his grandfather's possession of the throne.

To this the Yorkists, in their turn, had their answer ready. So be it! By right of custom Henry of Lancaster legitimately wears the crown; let him keep it during his lifetime. But after him it must return to him who is entitled to wear it by right of birth.

With his mind again badly shaken, anxious about his wife and his son, and above all passionately bent as always on restoring peace, the King did not have the strength to resist his enemies. He recognized the Duke of York as heir presumptive and annulled the claims of his own son. A second edict, wrung from him when he was unaware of what he was doing, ordered the Queen to return to London and bring the Prince of Wales with her, on pain of being denounced as a rebel.

Richard, while awaiting the succession, was again made Protector.

# ❧ 12 ❧

## *The Bloodstained Queen*

Upon learning that her son had been despoiled of his rights, Margaret gave way to one of those outbursts of violent feeling which were always pushing her towards disaster. In vain did her friends and advisers urge that it would be wise to give her partisans time to reorganize: she must hit back at once, and at any price! Since England was in no state to defend the rights of her princes, she would appeal for help to a foreigner, she would go to Scotland. To do anything of the kind was to stake Lancastrian chances on the throw of a dice. But it was not for nothing that Margaret was a daughter of both Aragon and Lorraine: she enjoyed taking gambles.

Braving autumn storms, pirates and Yorkist warships, she embarked with her son in the first ship that offered, and set sail. After a rough journey she reached Berwick, a scowling fortress which guarded the frontier. The Governor fortunately was an adherent of the Red Rose. From Berwick, overcoming a thousand difficulties, she reached Edinburgh.

King James II of Scotland had just died, killed at the siege of Roxburgh Castle. The new King, James III, was still an infant in arms, and his mother, Mary of Gelderland, was acting as regent. Margaret, counting on the old antagonism between the two nations, asked the Regent for help in reconquering her kingdom.

It is difficult, today, to form a clear idea of the bitter hatred which at that epoch of history, divided England and Scotland. It can best be compared to the hereditary hatred between two feuding Corsican families. Indeed, there was a centuries old vendetta between the two countries, fostered by the singing of bards and the playing of minstrels with that bloody hatred for their theme. In the border country a young Scot hardly considered himself a man until he had killed his first Englishman, or an English youth his first Scot. In regular warfare these perpetual enemies had measured their strength against each other in every possible battlefield, even on the banks of the Loire; but it was the almost daily border fighting and raiding which most heroically stirred the hearts of warriors on both sides. No less wild and warlike than the Lords, the clan chieftains were for ever leading fresh raids, attacking castles, rounding up and driving off flocks and herds, even stealing harvests and burning villages. These blood-stained giants, many of whom seemed to be nearer to cave men than to the Renaissance, compare with the terrible *Ecorcheurs*, the Flayers, the scourge of France. Their atrocious cruelty and half bestial ferocity were a by-word; their very name was used to frighten children who could not hear it without a cry of terror.

Such were the soldiers whom Margaret was asking the Queen Regent of Scotland to lend her, knowing with what savage joy they would hurl themselves at any English enemy. None but a woman driven to extremes by love for her child could have envisaged this appalling expedient without shrinking with horror. In France it had been traditional for malcontents to call in foreign troops to their aid. The English, more touchy in such matters, found this practice disgraceful; only four times in their history did they have recourse to it: in 1215 when the barons in revolt against John Lackland offered the throne to Philip-Augustus' son, the future Louis VIII; Margaret in

1460 when she called in the Scots and in 1462 when she called in the French; and in 1689 when James II tried to reconquer his throne with French aid.*

Margaret had no time to take such refinements of feeling into consideration. She may well have thought, like Francis I at the time of the signature of the Turkish capitulation, 'that when wolves were making their way into her house she certainly had the right to turn the dogs on them'.

The Regent Mary naturally put a price on Scottish help: she wanted Berwick, the major English bastion against Scotland, ceded to her. Margaret agreed, assembled her formidable army whose officers she had little difficulty in charming† and despite the season of the year, for it was in January 1461 that the treaty was arranged, opened her campaign.

As soon as Margaret was known to be back in England with a redoubtable army, the northern counties, devoted to the Lancastrian cause, rose in arms. Somerset and Clifford marched with the assembled Red Rose forces to join the Queen. In all the Queen now had 20,000 soldiers recruited from among the best fighting men in the world.

Past experience had taught her to rely on nobody but herself. Distrusting both the competence and the loyalty

---

* In France, on the other hand, examples are countless: 1214 the Emperor is called in by the barons; the English by the Armagnacs in 1413; the English by the Burgundians in 1419; by the Praguerie in 1442; by d'Alençon in 1455; by Saint-Pol and Le Téméraire in 1475. In 1523 the Constable de Bourbon prepared the way for Charles V's invasion. During the Wars of Religion the Protestants used English, the Catholics, Spanish, help. In 1627 La Rochelle called in Buckingham. All Richelieu's enemies, and later the Frondeurs treated with the foreigner. The great Condé commanded Spanish armies in France. And as for the *émigrés* . . .

† The Earls of Douglas and Angus seem to have been particularly susceptible. Chivalry was still a live force in Scotland and therefore to fight for a beautiful princess in trouble was bound to appeal to these knights. Incidentally, the House of Douglas was divided, the senior branch supporting the Lancastrians, while the cadet branch was for the White Rose of York.

of her captains—at Northampton those who had not turned traitor had not been up to their work—she decided to take personal command of her troops. This necessity made her a general of armies at thirty, just as it had made her a chief of state at seventeen. But then it was not the first time in that century that a princess of Lorraine had taken command of an army.

In a few days the Lancastrian forces reached York, in the heart of the enemy's own country. From that city Margaret issued a challenge to the Protector, and a solemn protestation against the Act which had disinherited her son. This assault and defiance surprised Richard, just at the moment when he felt assured that his victory was secure. He had been cleverer this time than he had been on either former occasion, and exploited the situation with the requisite, indeed indispensible, partiality. That is to say, without sparing any man, he had handed everything over to his friends, making very large-scale changes in the ownership of landed estates, and doing his best, even among the burgesses, to satisfy the many at the expense of the few. By so doing he bound large and very powerful interests to his government. There is nothing like economic considerations for undermining convictions and loyalties based on other considerations: those for whom a Lancastrian victory would now mean heavy losses or even ruin, became ardent champions of the legitimacy of the Yorkist cause.

This state of affairs had very greatly enhanced the Protector's confidence in his star. As a consequence, he began by laughing at that horde of Scottish brigands under the command of a woman. And yet, he himself was hardly in a position to fight them, his own troops, gorged on the spoils of victory, having been disbanded several months ago. He could hardly muster an army of 5,000 or 6,000 men. On Salisbury's advice he decided to put himself at the head of this little army and take up a position on the road to London so as to bar the invader's route to the capital. Meanwhile Warwick would guard the City and the King, while the Earl of March was busy reassembling the White Rose tenants.

The Duke therefore entrenched himself with Rutland, his fifteen-year-old second son, Salisbury, and their knights, in Sandal Castle, one of those prodigious fortresses which England had put on like armour following the Conquest, and beside which the French Gisors or Tarascon look like bungalows. There he could safely hold on for weeks, until reinforcements arrived.

Meanwhile the terrible Borderers were flowing over and devastating the North like a flood of lava from a volcano, leaving behind them a trail of corpses and burning villages and farms. The terrorized peasants, abandoning home and land, fled before them.

The Yorkists, needless to say, seized upon these events with gusto, posing as the nation's champions against these hairy barbarians led by the foreign woman whose evil designs they had so long and tirelessly denounced. At this juncture Margaret could well have done with a little more hypocrisy. Her adversaries had never shrunk from imposing monstrous exactions when they got the chance. Warwick had proved that. But they always took the wise precaution of giving a handsome appearance even to their least excusable excesses by protesting their patriotic devotion to the public welfare and national interest. Their arguments might often be crude, but they were, as a rule, quite good enough, well-designed to flatter the illusions of the multitude.

Disdaining such devices, the Queen, on the other hand, appeared by comparison to be acting selfishly and without any regard for the country's welfare.

The Lancastrians encamped about the little town of Wakefield at the foot of Sandal Castle. As they had no artillery, their position was not a good one. To force

Richard into the open the Queen tried to exasperate his pride, and for three days in succession had him challenged by a herald in insulting terms. The most elementary prudence should have kept Richard safe within his fortifications. But rage and braggadocio blinded him just as Talbot had been blinded by pride at Castillon. Finally, on 21 December 1460, he let himself be provoked into a pitched battle.

Margaret herself superintended the placing of her troops and the order of battle. Perhaps she had read her Livy, for her tactics on this occasion have all the appearance of being inspired by Hannibal's at Cannae. As the centre of the Red Rose army deliberately gave way before the Yorkist charge, the Lancastrian horse, concealed behind a rise of land, turned the enemy's flank and took him in the rear. At the same time the companies at the centre, disposed in depth, divided and over-ran both the enemy flanks. Thus surrounded on all sides, the White Rose knights lost their footing, faltered, and in a few minutes their defeat became a rout, and then a massacre. Orders had been issued to the Lancastrian forces to spare none but the leaders, the rest were to be killed. Clifford distinguished himself by his ferocity: he sacrificed literally dozens of men to the memory of his father. On Wakefield bridge he caught up with the young Lord Rutland, fleeing the field with his preceptor, who pleaded in vain for the boy's life: savagely, Clifford killed both of them with his own hand.

Salisbury, wounded, was captured, as were numerous Yorkist lords. The Protector, resolved never to fall into his enemy's hands, fought gallantly until he was killed. Clifford, finding his body, cut off the head and carried it to the Queen, whom he found reviewing the prisoners who had been dragged before her.

Where now was the once gentle Margaret? Where the divine princess destined to become the heroine of poetic legends? In her place stood an Amazon drunk on the stench of blood and gunpowder and the harsh taste of vengeance. Tragically, she was made mad by the memory of sufferings past. She would exact payment now, to the last farthing—payment for Suffolk's death and Somerset's and the deaths of so many loyal friends; payment for the foul calumnies on the birth of the Prince of Wales; payment for the outrages inflicted on the King; for her own flights from the enemy, her spoilation by the robbers; payment for the insolence of Parliament, and for ten years of intolerable humiliation.

At the sight of Richard of York's blood-stained head, the Queen laughed aloud and struck it in the face. And she ordered that Salisbury and the other prisoners be instantly beheaded.

Even that did not calm her fury, or slake her thirst for revenge. Derisively, she had a paper crown placed on Richard's severed head and had it set, with Salisbury's, stuck on pikes, on the walls of York. Between the two heads were set two more pikes: they were for Warwick, said the Queen, and the Earl of March.

For thirty years the Wars of the Roses were to be rich in atrocities. Edward IV was, in due course, greatly to surpass both Clifford and Margaret in cruelty. Yet the Wakefield executions seemed to have made much the deepest impression on the imagination of the mass of the people, both then and later. Certainly Margaret's reputation never recovered from them, and even today her memory bears a terrible blemish because of them. After Wakefield she became and has remained the Bloody Queen.

Why did posterity damn her with that terrible curse, a curse which both Edward and Warwick and a score of other butchers earned but were spared? Because on that dreadful day the vanquished were, for the first time, handed over to the executioner? Because the tragedy of a bloody massacre seems even worse if ordered by a woman?

Possibly: but also because the White Rose was so much more deft at pleading its cause and turning its enemy's fame into infamy.

Thus Shakespeare, over 100 years later, gave Margaret a personal hand in the death of Richard of York, in a scene heavily slanted against the Queen:

*Queen Margaret*. Brave warriors, Clifford and Northumberland,
    Come make him stand upon this molehill here,
    That raught at mountains with outstretched arms,
    Yet parted but the shadow with his hand.
    What, was it you that would be England's king?
    Was't you that revell'd in our parliament
    And made a preachment of your high descent?
    Where are your mess of sons to back you now—
    The wanton Edward and the lusty George?
    And where's that valiant crook-back prodigy,
    Dicky your boy, that with his grumbling voice
    Was wont to cheer his dad in mutinies?
    Or, with the rest, where is your darling Rutland?
    Look, York: I stain'd this napkin with the blood
    That valiant Clifford with his rapier's point
    Made issue from the bosom of the boy:
    And if thine eyes water for his death,
    I give thee this to dry thy cheeks withal.
    Alas, poor York! but that I hate thee deadly,
    I should lament thy miserable state.
    I prithee grieve, to make me merry, York.
    What, hath thy fiery heart so parch'd thine entrails
    That not a tear can fall for Rutland's death?
    Why art thou patient, man? thou should'st be mad;
    And I to make thee mad do mock thee thus.
    Stamp, rave, and fret, that I may sing and dance.
    Thou would'st be fee'd, I see, to make me sport;
    York cannot speak unless he wear a crown.

A crown for York! and, lords, bow low to him:
Hold you his hands whilst I do set it on.

                    *[Putting a paper crown on his head.]*
Ay, marry, sir, now looks he like a king!
Ay, this is he that took King Henry's chair,
And this is he was his adopted heir.
But how is it that great Plantagenet
Is crown'd so soon and broke his solemn oath?
As I bethink me, you should not be king
Till our King Henry had shook hands with Death.
And will you pale your head in Henry's glory,
And rob his temples of the diadem,
Now in his life, against your holy oath?
O, 'tis a fault too too unpardonable!
Off with the crown, and, with the crown, his head;
And, whilst we breathe, take time to do him dead.
*Clifford.* That is my office, for my father's sake.
*Queen Margaret.* Nay, stay; let's hear the orisons he makes.
*York.* She-wolf of France, but worse than wolves of France,
Whose tongue more poisons than the adder's tooth!
How ill-beseeming is it in thy sex
To triumph like an Amazonian trull
Upon their woes whom Fortune captivates!
But that thy face is vizard-like, unchanging,
Made impudent with use of evil deeds,
I would assay, proud queen, to make thee blush.
To tell thee whence thou cam'st, of whom deriv'd,
Were shame enough to shame thee, wert not shameless.
Thy father bears the type of King of Naples,
Of both the Sicils, and Jerusalem,
Yet not so wealthy as an English yeoman.
Hath that poor monarch taught thee to insult?
It needs not, nor it boots thee not, proud queen;
Unless the adage must be verified,
That beggars mounted run their horse to death.
'Tis beauty that doth oft make women proud;

But God he knows thy share thereof is small.
'Tis virtue that doth make them most admir'd;
The contrary doth make thee wonder'd at.
'Tis government that makes them seem divine;
The want thereof makes thee abominable.
Thou art as opposite to every good
As the Antipodes are unto us,
Or as the south to the Septentrion.
O tiger's heart wrapp'd in a woman's hide!
How could'st thou drain the life-blood of the child,
To bid the father wipe his eyes withal,
And yet be seen to bear a woman's face?
Women are soft, mild, pitiful, and flexible;
Thou stern, indurate, flinty, rough, remorseless.
Bid'st thou me rage? Why, now thou hast thy wish.
Would'st have me weep? Why, now thou hast thy will.
For raging wind blows up incessant showers,
And when the rage allays, the rain begins.
These tears are my sweet Rutland's obsequies,
And every drop cries vengeance for his death
'Gainst thee, fell Clifford, and thee, false French-
     woman.
*Northumberland.* Beshrew me, but his passion moves me so
     As hardly can I check my eyes from tears.
*York.* That face of his the hungry cannibals
     Would not have touch'd, would not have stain'd with
          blood;
     But you are more inhuman, more inexorable—
     O, ten times more—than tigers of Hyrcania.
     See, ruthless queen, a hapless father's tears.
     This cloth thou dipp'd'st in blood of my sweet boy,
     And I with tears do wash the blood away.
     Keep thou the napkin, and go boast of this;
     And if thou tell the heavy story right,
     Upon my soul, the hearers will shed tears;
     Yea, even my foes will shed fast-falling tears,

And say 'Alas! it was a piteous deed.'
There, take the crown, and with the crown my curse;
And in thy need such comfort come to thee
As now I reap at thy too cruel hand!
Hard-hearted Clifford, take me from the world:
My soul to heaven, my blood upon your heads!

*Northumberland.* Had he been slaughter-man to all my kin
I should not for my life but weep with him,
To see how inly sorrow gripes his soul.

*Queen Margaret.* What, weeping-ripe, my lord Northumber-
land?
Think but upon the wrong he did us all,
And that will quickly dry thy melting tears.

*Clifford.* Here's for my oath, here's for my father's death.
*Stabbing him.*

*Queen Margaret.* And here's to right our gentle-hearted
king.
*Stabbing him.*

*York.* Open thy gate of mercy, gracious God!
My soul flies through these wounds to seek out Thee.
*Dies.*

*Queen Margaret.* Off with his head, and set it on York gates;
So York may overlook the town of York.
*Flourish. Exeunt.*

(3 Henry VI, I. iv)

It was the Queen's misfortune that after Wakefield she had
no money to reward her ruffians, and that this want of
money made itself felt at the very moment when she was
herself setting them so baleful an example. She could not
prevent her army from looting the whole countryside or
from spreading horror and panic. As a result peasant and
burgess alike fled to enlist under Warwick and the Earl of
March, who were both advancing with armies, bent on

avenging their fathers' deaths. Margaret should, of course, have kept her forces together in one body. As it was, she made the mistake of dividing them into two armies. The first, led by Owen Tudor, was to intercept and check the momentum of the youthful Edward's advance; the other, commanded by herself, was to march on London, brushing Warwick aside.

On 1 February 1461, the Earl of March and the Tudors met at Mortimer's Cross. That was Edward's first victory. The defeated Lancastrians beat a hasty retreat, leaving Owen Tudor and his principal lieutenants in enemy hands. Edward Plantagenet was then twenty years of age. His striking physical beauty and his knightly courage so predisposed people in his favour, that he was credited with all the virtues. In point of fact, however, he had all the vices of his blood, and at times they were evident in full measure, notably that cold cruelty which was to find its ultimate expression in fratricide.

Edward's prisoners were put to death: and thus died, among the rest, Owen Tudor, that gallant little Welsh squire, husband of a queen and father of the stock from which sprang England's most powerful dynasty.*

On receiving the news of the victory, Warwick quickened his march. Not daring to leave his precious hostage behind, he brought Henry, wretched, pathetic and resigned, with him.

His meeting with the army of the Red Rose took place at St Albans on 17 February 1461, the same site as the

---

\* By Catherine of Valois he had two sons, Edmund and Jaspar. Edmund, Earl of Richmond, died young after marrying Margaret Beaufort, a daughter of the first Duke of Somerset who was the Constable's eldest brother. He had a son, born after Edmund's death, Henry, who became King Henry VII. This family's case poses a very curious problem. To the husband she did not love, Catherine bore a puny, sickly son who was feeble minded. To her lover she bore two splended, healthy children and her issue was the vigorous race distinguished by Henry VIII and Elizabeth I. See the genealogical tables at the end of this volume.

first battle in the war. On that day Margaret proved that
the will to serve the cause of a beloved son can make a
great military strategist of a woman. Totally defeated, the
great earl was forced to beat a disorderly retreat; and,
worst blow of all, to leave the King in Margaret's hands.
He did, however, succeed in effecting a junction with
Edward.

After a separation lasting a whole year, Henry and his
wife were at last able to clasp each other in their arms, and
to shed tears of affection and happiness. The King dubbed
his son knight. At eight years old, the Prince of Wales was
already a bold, brave lad, following the course of his
mother's battles without showing fear. But even while
these touching domestic scenes were being enacted, in
St Albans itself the spectacle was an atrocious one.
Margaret's troops, completely out of hand, were murder-
ing their prisoners, looting, raping and wantonly burning.
Horror at what happened in St Albans spread throughout
the kingdom. It was in vain that the Queen, who realized
the danger, poured out reassuring proclamations and
promises of amnesty. It was rumoured that the men of the
North, for centuries jealous of southern prosperity, had
sworn to leave a desert behind them.

All southern England rose in arms; Edward and Warwick, now looked upon as their countrymen's last hope of
salvation, made their way back to London. When the
Lancastrian army reached the city, they found its gates
closed and its walls bristling with cannon, and by way of
venting their spleen, ravaged and looted the surrounding
country.

Their excesses had one decisive consequence: they gave
the Crown to Edward, Earl of March. On 4 March 1461
Parliament solemnly proclaimed Richard of York's son
'King of France and of England, Prince of Wales, and
Lord of Ireland' under the name and title Edward IV.

Margaret did not have enough soldiers to lay siege to

London. She withdrew, calling upon all Lancaster's liegemen to rally to her standard, and asking the Regent, Mary of Scotland, for reinforcements. Crowds of knights arrived from the northern counties, and another horde of Scots came swarming down from their glens and mountains, until the Queen had 60,000 men under her colours, a larger army than Henry V or the Black Prince had ever commanded.

Meanwhile in London the tocsin was calling all men, no longer to a duel between two factions of the Lords, a mere dynastic quarrel, but to a crusade, a holy war to protect hearth and home, property and family, against the hereditary enemy. At the heart of an army composed of men rendered heroic by the need to defend their own, Edward marched against the Queen. On 28 March 1461, the eve of Palm Sunday, in and about the villages of Towton and Saxton, between the rivers Warf and Cock, began a battle which lasted for forty hours and was the bloodiest fought in the century. The weather was appalling, with snow being driven by a gale of wind, a cruel blizzard; at noon it was as dark as midnight, and the soldiers could barely see the enemy they were killing.

At the end of the first day, after a brilliant offensive led by Clifford, the advantage lay with Lancaster and the Yorkist army was beginning to melt away. The movement was checked by Warwick's theatrical gesture when, stabbing his own horse to the heart with his sword, he swore an oath on the cross of that same sword that on that battlefield he would either vanquish or die. Rallying the troops, he counter-attacked furiously, forced Clifford to fall back from the ground he had won, and killed him with his own hand.*

The army of the Red Rose gave ground but did not

---

* Clifford's son fled to escape Yorkist vengeance, hiding in the countryside disguised as a shepherd. For a quarter of a century, until the advent of Henry VII, he maintained this disguise.

retreat, and all through the night and the following day
the slaughter continued. The gale became even more
temptestuous, and drove the heavily falling snow into the
faces of the Lancastrians. But until evening they fought
on, striking blindly, slipping and staggering in the blood-
stained mire. For a while when they were almost exhausted
they seemed to be holding the enemy, even forcing him on
the defensive. But Yorkist reinforcements appeared and
the Queen's men began to fall back, retreating towards
the river. Over-burdened, the bridges gave way; the
Yorkist cavalry attacked again, and there followed one of
the worst massacres in the history of war.

When Monday's dawn shone through the clouds,
36,000 corpses lay on the battlefield; of these 28,000 were
Lancaster's dead and the rivers Cock and Warf still ran
red with blood.


Once again Margaret and those with her fled, seeking
refuge in Scotland. After such losses, such failures, such
unrewarded striving as had been hers, any other woman
would have bowed to the verdict of fate and accepted
defeat. The Queen had many friends among the Scottish
lords who admired her heroism and her beauty. The
Regent Mary offered her a castle where, with her husband
and her son, she could have spent her days in tranquillity
and devoted herself to the young Prince's education. But
Margaret was incapable of moderating her feelings: while
she had a breath of life in her body, she would fight to
win the crown for her son.

But the Regent, alarmed by defeat, categorically refused
to embark on another such adventure; and Margaret, past
weighing up the dangers of such a course, now turned to
her own family, to Charles VII.

A small delegation of Lancastrians led by the Duke of
Somerset went to France, hoping to enlist Charles's

sympathy for his niece's plight. Unfortunately, by the time this embassy landed in France, Charles was in no position to help, having died on 22 July 1461. The new King was the terrible Dauphin Louis, later to be known as the 'Spider King'.

Being hardly established on a throne which he seemed to owe as much to the Duke of Burgundy as to his right, with a mountain of business and a thousand difficulties and dangers confronting him, Louis XI could not even dream of interfering in the English civil war. First cousin to Henry VI through his aunt, Catherine, and to Margaret through his mother, Marie of Anjou, he had very little use for either of them. He distrusted the Lancasters as the Duke of Burgundy's kinsmen; and as for the House of Anjou, he had two reasons for disliking it: it had far too much feudal power; and he nursed an old grudge against King René who, by refusing to support his nephew when he rebelled against Charles VII, had been instrumental in forcing him into exile. King Louis was not the man to forgive trespasses against the Dauphin Louis.

Anxious to avoid compromising himself, he had Margaret's ambassadors thrown into prison, and the Queen had the greatest difficulty in getting them set at liberty. She then realized that she would have to go herself to France to see her redoubtable cousin. With no thought of the risk she was running, in April 1462 she set out on that terrible journey.

Experience having taught her to protect herself even against her best friends, she was unwilling to leave her husband in Scotland. Who could be sure that someone would not try to make political use of the sick King? So, Henry having been entrusted to the fortifications of Harlech Castle, the Queen looked for a ship, finding one through the good offices of a merchant to whom she had been helpful in the past.

Aboard that small and indifferent vessel, with her son

and a handful of servants, she set sail for France. She had left it seventeen years ago, bound for love, regality, happiness and power. What now remained to her? Like Corneille's Medea, Margaret might have answered:

'Myself, and that suffices!'

# BOOK THREE

# The Hurricane

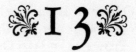

# King Louis XI

In the year 1462 France seemed to be encircled by some mysterious and fearsome disturbance. No man could yet foresee its nature, but a hundred signs and omens presaged its menacing approach. The air seemed full of the tension, the uneasiness which foreruns a storm.

For thirty years, two rival and incompatible powers, driven towards collision by the rising storm of events, had both been gathering an alarming momentum. A clash was becoming daily more inevitable.

On the one hand there was regality, driving roots which were remarkably stout deep into the soil of France. Royal victories over the English, the close communion between King and people, and a constellation of brilliant agents, had given the Crown an authority and a prestige hitherto unknown, and such that princes in difficulties with their people, or their families, were soon to be resorting to Louis XI as arbiter. No French King since Charlemagne, says Chastellain writing of this epoch, was so well obeyed and well served as King Louis.

On the other hand, there was the provincial power of the great feudatories and their semi-independent fiefs, and of the apanagist princes. As regality gained strength in depth, these latter gained in extent. The King was powerful but on an island, an island beset on north and east by the

Duke of Burgundy, on the west by the Duke of Brittany, in the south by the Duke of Bourbon, the Count of Provence and the Duke of Savoy, not to mention a host of lesser nobles, all fat with lands and privileges, and all unsatisfied, greedy for more. Despite the extent of their domains, their *de facto* independence and the central strong points of their fortress-castles, they were aware of the royal power steadily undermining their own. And to ensure themselves against the risk of explosion, each of them coveted something more, demanded this or that.

Philip the Good, grown old now, his interests divided between his family and his favourites, the Croys, a flemish family, was slowly relinquishing the reins of government. But his son the Count of Charolais, harking back to the dream of John the Fearless, was in quest of a crown. The House of Anjou alone claimed five crowns—the two Sicilies, Aragon, Majorca, Cyprus and Jerusalem. The Duke of Berry, the King's brother, was demanding an immense apanage, analogous to that of John the Good's sons. The Bourbons, the Luxembourgs, the Dunois, the bastards of scores of noble houses, all wanted places, money, benefices.

And the King—what did he want? There was a brief moment when the great and little nobles had thought they might be celebrating their own advent when they celebrated that of the poor Dauphin who had arrived in Paris in the Duke of Burgundy's baggage train and was crowned in Reims by Philip the Good himself. Louis seemed to have decided to destroy this illusion from the moment when, during his coronation feast, he had sent a plebian giant into the tourney lists, who had made short work of his knightly opponents.

Now, surrounding himself in this same spirit with nameless men—Bische, Phillipe Pot and the like—and dressed like a villein, Louis was again indulging his 'strangeness and subtleties'. So eager was he to begin the struggle, so impatient to start reforming, innovating, acquiring, that he forgot all prudence, all moderation. He attacked everything simultaneously—Aragon, the Milanese, the Pragmatic Sanctions, the financiers. Slap after slap in the face was administered to the great feudal lords: one day by enobling men engaged in trade; on another—with almost crazy bravado—by reserving all hunting rights for the Crown. A King of France who was prepared to go to such lengths must feel himself to be very strong. But in reality, Louis was not strong, not while the Duke of Burgundy held him by the throat with his occupation of the Somme towns—Amiens, Doullens, Péronne, Saint-Quentin—which had been ceded by Charles VII at the Treaty of Arras; nor while England still held a loaded weapon pressed to France's chest—Calais. It only needed a reconciliation between the two old allies, France's enemies, and within two days they could be in Paris. At any too abrupt political movement, the King felt this sword of Damocles tremble above his head. No really great undertaking was possible so long as England remained potentially dangerous.

All of which Louis understood perfectly well. One of his first acts, as soon as he had Somerset under lock and key, was to send an envoy to Edward IV with proposals for a permanent peace. But the victor of Towton rejected them contemptuously.

The best way to establish a new dynasty firmly is to vindicate it by waging a successful war. The Yorkists were well aware of this and were already talking openly of reconquering their kingdom of France. And the people cheered. England was poor now, almost ruined by the civil war, unable even to get enough wine since the loss of Aquitaine; she could not look without envy at her rival's rich provinces across the Channel and the memory of profitable raids in the past made Englishmen's mouths water. Under pressure of public opinion, Edward openly announced his intention to invade France soon. As early as March the ports were noisy with shipbuilders' adzes and armourers' hammers, and these bellicose preparations were on a scale worthy of the Trojan War. The Duke of Brittany and the Count of Charolais were already secretly congratulating themselves and imagining just how they would oblige their dear cousin of England to grant them a part of his spoils.

It was in the midst of these threatening precursors of the gathering storm that in April 1462 Margaret of Anjou, deposed Queen of England, again set foot on French soil. It seemed that her presence in that centre of so many interwoven intrigues and clashing ambitions must be very welcome to men always so ready to seize the least opportunity to interfere in other people's business. But if that was, indeed, the hope she was entertaining, she was not long in discovering how wrong she had been.

And her first discovery was that she could hope for nothing from the Angevins. King René, indeed, received her with all the tenderness of a father reunited with an unhappy daughter after a long separation. But what could he do for her? The older he became, the less his inclination to meddle personally in any kind of political complication. His love for his young wife Jeanne de Laval, his pastorals, his tourneys, and the experiments of his alchemists absorbed all his time and attention. Ever since the accession of his nephew who, as René was aware, detested him, he had kept away from the court. Moreover, he was still only nominally head of the House of Anjou: the family ambition and energy were not to be found in him, but in his eldest son, John, Duke of Calabria.

How charming and picturesque a figure he cuts, the young Angevin prince—adventurous, a *conquistador* without a conquest, a Knight Errant for ever unlucky in his

ventures, but unwearying, tirelessly riding the roads of
all Europe in his search for chimerical empires. A worthy
son of his mother, a worthy brother of his sister, he had
just set out again on the Italian venture, and gone to join
his partisans in Italy. The family's last resources were all
invested in this great expedition; there was certainly
nothing to spare for the Lancasters.

There was still the King: on the eve of facing a new
English invasion, surely his policy must be to try and
paralyse the enemy. And what better way could there be
than that of helping to restore the fortunes of the Red
Rose?

But, in the event, it was not his cousin Margaret whom
the crafty monarch wanted as an ally. A nature like his was
never at ease with, could never understand such downright, intransigent, catagorical natures as his cousin's, to
whom all shifts and concessions and lies were alien. He
preferred to have dealings with rascally intriguers, two-
faced men with an eye to the main chance, rapaciously
ambitious men with whom one could make an underhand
deal. And Louis had found just such a man, an inter-
locutor wholly to his taste, in the Earl of Warwick. The
Great Earl knew to a scruple the weight of gratitude in the
hearts of princes. Thus he judged it not inopportune to
ensure abroad a measure of support which, in case of need,
might serve to preserve Edward IV from the sin of
ingratitude.

Another consideration made the same conduct expedient: his big piracy and smuggling business relied on the
neutrality of the Norman corsairs. Futhermore, France's
friendship was an insurance against a Lancastrian come-
back. There was a final and supreme argument for an
understanding with Louis: Warwick was very fond of
money. His house, his livery, his ships, his enormous
following of clients and his countless castles, swallowed
millions. All this magnificence was the foundation of his

political fortune: and Charles VII's coffers, Louis XI's legacy, were overflowing with gold. Miserly at home, Louis could be prodigal when the national interest required prodigality. He became a sleeping partner in Warwick's undertakings, investing in the Earl's power.

Whence his feeling of security, his carefree attitude at the very moment when he was expecting an attack by an armada; it would be an armada led by his partner, by a man beholden to him. Far from giving thought to his defences, he went on a careful probing progress through his realm, remote from the threatened coast; and spent time haggling with the King of Aragon over a loan for which Roussillon was to be the pledge.

One of his objects was to avoid the importunate Queen, but Margaret pursued him tenaciously, for weeks, from castle to castle, begging help from everyone—her aunt, the Queen Mother, Marie of Anjou, ministers, officers, trying everything from charm to pathos in her appeal.

Louis XI was a gambler, so passionate a gambler that he readily staked bets on several different chances at the same time. He began to think of some way to make something for himself out of his cousin's misfortunes.

Margaret's circumstances made her an easy prey. Everyone was sorry for their ruined kinswoman—and was careful to avoid her. England's Queen was reduced to selling her jewellery and begging small subsidies from her father. To her humiliation was added horror at the prospect of seeing the Prince of Wales an exile living in poverty. To that she would never resign herself; she would have sold her soul to the devil for the chance to resume the struggle.

And the devil duly appeared to tempt her: the King sent to say that he would receive her at the Château d'Amboise in May 1462.

Nearly eighteen years had passed since the cousins had last seen each other. Both made a great show of affection;

and each watched the other with distrust, astonishment and curiosity.

Sickly, his back almost hunched, and with legs too weak for his body—a legacy from his father—Louis was weasel-faced; yet his countenance was sometimes illuminated with a strange genius. He wore the ostentatiously simple clothes which were an element of the 'image' which he had chosen and was deliberately creating. Not yet a great King, he had long been a bad-hearted, ill-natured man; and the implications of this evil reputation made his presence vaguely sinister. He was said to have poisoned his first wife, Margaret Stuart, and Agnes Sorel; even the death of his father, killed from a distance by a sort of terror and grief maintained by some diabolical means was imputed to Louis. And in an age when atrocities in war surprised nobody, his cruelties during his campaigns in Switzerland had attracted horrified attention.

Margaret did her best to soften the heart of this enigmatic and icy-hearted man, to move him with her beauty. Her fine words slid off the King's smooth amiability like water off an oiled surface. However, Louis was very free with words of compassion and promises of friendship, and seemed genuinely to be seeking a means to be of use to her.

He liked making loans against pledges; it was an expedient which enabled him to oblige his friends while saving appearances. His 'lovely cousin' was short of money and soldiers, was she? Well, then, he could advance her 20,000 *livres*, and authorize her to raise a small army among French Knights with an appetite for glory and adventure. But he would have to ask her for a pledge which would ensure the recovery of his capital, with the usual interest. What pledge had he in mind?

Calais.

*Calais après trois cents quarante jours de siège,*
*Fut sur Valois vaincu, conquis par les Anglais.*

> *Quand le plomb flottera sur l'eau comme la liège,*
> *Les Valois reprendront sur les Anglais, Calais.* *

That proud quatrain, carved on the brow of the fortress, gives only a feeble notion of the love which the English felt for their Calais. Calais was at once the island's shield and gateway, mistress of the straits, guardian of sea-borne trade, open door into the Continent, tangible token that a future reconquest was always possible. Still more, it was the symbol of former victories, a banner proudly planted in enemy country. For so long as they held Calais, the English had not really lost the war.

How could Margaret envisage handing over her people's dearest treasure, wiping out their most cherished hope? Were she to do so she would be justifying all the slanders, rebellions and persecutions of her enemies, and making outlaws of the Lancasters. Seeking a way out, she declared herself in no position to hand over a town firmly held by Warwick who would, if he had to, defend the place with desperate courage and determination. Besides, would not such a promise for ever close England to Henry VI?

But her terrible cousin Louis had his answers ready. Margaret need only undertake to appoint a man they could rely upon as Governor of Calais—say the Earl of Pembroke, or Thomas de Foix, Earl of Kendal. The moment the Lancasters were again masters of their realm, the French would attack Calais. God and the Governor aiding, perhaps it might be granted to them to capture the citadel after a siege less long than that of 1347. By this means not even the most captious critic could find anything to reproach her with.

The poor woman felt herself caught in a trap. She also

---

* Calais after three hundred and forty days of siege,
  Was from vanquished Valois, conquered by the English.
  When lead shall float on water like cork
  The Valois will take Calais back from the English.

realized that, once she had given this pledge, not all the gold in the world would suffice to redeem it. Such a sacrifice was impossible: she could not load her son with the burden of such a felony, could not hand her enemies proof positive that the Lancasters did not hesitate to put their personal ambitions above the country's interests. And for all she knew, this crowned knave was trying to trap her at Warwick's instigation, seeking to dishonour her for the benefit of the White Rose.

But then what was she to do? If she rejected the shameful bargain, would her last chance be any less utterly lost? And one royal thief might be caught by another. The art of diplomacy in the fifteenth century consisted in making treaties whose more troublesome clauses could, when the time came, always be forgotten. Once she had reconquered the throne, the Queen would cast around for some means of breaking her word elegantly. If she accepted the proposed bargain, there were some terrible prospects ahead; but to refuse it meant immediate and final failure.

Margaret shut her eyes and jumped into the abyss: on 23 June 1462 she agreed. In exchange she received 20,000 *livres* and 2,000 men at arms mustered without much difficulty.

The Queen could not always be a general commanding armies; she needed a man to take command of her soldiers. She asked the King to give her Brézé.

Pierre de Brézé, born a vassal of René d'Anjou, had served—some even say ruled—Charles VII with passionate devotion. Rightly was he called the most complete man of his day. Soldier, diplomat and administrator, he was, like Richemont, Jacques Coeur and the Bureau brothers, one of the number of admirable public servants to whom the Kingdom of France owed its revival. The great military reform, the creation of the corps of *francs-archers*, free bowmen, was his work. Either more adroit or more modest than others, he had managed never to offend his master, and to retain his confidence, although Charles never really liked him. The Seneschalcy of Poitou, then of Normandy, a seat in the Council, the county of Auxerre and its titles, and some large endowments were the payment for his services.

At court and in the army there was no man more brilliant. 'Where the sword could not prevail, his tongue vanquished.' And it was said that ladies could no more resist him than his adversaries defeat him.

At the time when the Dauphin's conduct was threatening France with civil war, Brézé was one of his opponents and the direct cause of his exile. In 1446 the prince had tried to have him assassinated; and he swore that on the morrow of his accession to the crown, the Seneschal's head should fall. When Charles VII died, Brézé's friends advised him to flee the country. The Count had shrugged his shoulders, knowing that the monarchy would always have need of men of his temper and mettle. Boldly, therefore, he presented himself before Louis XI; the King did not at first respond in kind to the nobility of Brézé's attitude, but had his enemy shut up in the terrible prison of Loches castle. But he was not, of course, unaware of the worth of this great servant of the Crown; and happy to find an opportunity to wipe out the past and to make use of his father's minister while removing him to a distance from court, he readily granted Margaret's request.

She, therefore, had the joy of being responsible for Brézé's liberation and even for getting his old commands restored to him. Restored to his Seneschaly, the Count made a triumphal progress through Normandy, greeted everywhere by the cheers of a deliriously enthusiastic people.

Despite all her vicissitudes the Queen had never forgotten the magnificent gentleman, who had been the first to offer himself as her Knight, as he had been the first to stir her heart and senses. Now, at the age of fifty-four, he was still in the flower of his strength and manly beauty, while she, at thirty-two, was still an incomparably beautiful woman, her beauty made all the more moving by the marks of suffering which her trials had left on her.

At the very moment when she felt herself helpless, not knowing where to turn next, utterly alone, threatened by dangers on all sides, at the mercy of other men's cowardice and cunning, she found in a love revived after fifteen years a last moment of happiness and forgetfulness.

# ❧14❧

## Hexham Forest

Despite the wish of both parties to keep their negotiations secret, the fact that Louis XI and his cousin were negotiating was very soon known in England, where it provoked an outcry which we might call an explosion of nationalism.

Warwick realized the need to feed this fury, and at the same time to put himself above suspicion, for his own contacts with France were not unknown. There was a possibility that he might be accused of having some hand in any machinations against Calais, of which he was governor. Resounding challenges were exchanged between Edward IV and Louis XI; but as this rodomontade did nothing to stop the British lion from growling furiously, Warwick at last made up his mind to put the expeditionary force, which had been mustered since the spring, into action.

So in August 1462 the great fleet sailed under the command of the Lord High Admiral. Not for forty years had England seen such a splended warlike array, so many ships, archers and knights. The day of England's recovery and revenge had come, and no longer would the lilies of France on Edward's blazon be a mockery.

But instead of a conquest, the world was treated to the spectacle of a maritime procession: Warwick gave his fleet and army an agreeable cruise down the French coast. The towns they passed were, indeed, garrisoned; but although these garrisons were much reduced, the Admiral considered them all too dangerous to be faced. After some weeks of this pleasure cruise, he finally made up his mind to ravage a countryside. Oddly enough this was not properly in France, but in Brittany, whose Duke was King Louis' enemy. After which, proud of this exploit, the Earl led his fleet back into harbour.

The straits were clear of warships. Without losing a moment, Margaret, the Prince of Wales, Brézé and their knights embarked in a dozen small ships and scuttled across to England on 9 October 1462.

This expedition, to which the Queen had sacrificed Lancastrian honour, was short and disastrous. The Queen wanted to land at Tynemouth where she believed she had friends. But its Governor, loyal to Edward IV, received the flotilla with cannon fire. To add to its miseries, a storm blew up, wrecked some of the ships and scattered the rest. A part of the stores, the money borrowed at such a fearful price, went to the bottom. Some of the French soldiers managed to land or were cast away on a small island off the coast. Soon surrounded by Yorkist troops, they were wiped out.

Overcoming a thousand difficulties, the Queen, the Seneschal and a remnant of their following succeeded in reaching Berwick, now a Scottish town. Far from being cast down they busied themselves in mustering what strength they could. Learning that Margaret was back, Somerset and his two brothers, Edmund and John Beaufort, accompanied by numerous lords of the Red Rose, hastened to join her. Poor Henry was fetched from Harlech to Berwick. The Regent of Scotland granted a modicum of aid.

Followed, during the next several months, a series of careful, small scale operations confined to the northern counties. Too weak to risk a battle, the Lancastrians waged a guerilla war of attrition, capturing a castle one day, a hamlet or village the next, progressing little by little but not ineffectively. By the spring of 1463 they had established a sound strategic base. As soon as reinforcements arrived they would be in a position to go over to the offensive; with one of the first soldiers in Europe as their general, they might hope for success.

Their internal dissensions ruined everything.

Henry Beaufort, Duke of Somerset, had inherited from his father a spirit devoid of nobility, all too prone to be positively ignoble. Like many of the officers in the army he was secretly in love with the Queen, or at least had designs on her. The absence of any favoured rival had enabled him to keep his feelings under control, but becoming aware of the intimacy between Margaret and Brézé, he lost his self-control and in a wild fit of jealousy, this son of the man responsible for the war, and natural leader of the Red Rose, turned his coat and went over to the White Rose taking several of his friends with him, including the young Duke of Suffolk. At the same time these renegades delivered Bamborough Castle, key to the Lancastrian position, into enemy hands.

He soon had cause to regret it. Once assured of the fruits of Somerset's treason, the Yorkists, contemptuous of the traitor, refused to pay the pension they had promised him. Somerset's eyes were opened then by remorse and he flew to cast himself at the Queen's feet. Margaret forgave him, less out of clemency than from necessity.

Despite these divisions the Red Rose, thanks to Brézé, grew stronger day by day. Edward and Warwick resolved to have done with it, marched with a powerful army and forced the Lancastrians to give battle in the skirts of Hexham forest. Margaret had joined her army, leaving Henry VI in Berwick. They never saw each other again. But the Prince of Wales accompanied his mother, who could not bear to let him be far away from her for long.

In spite of the very great inequality of the two armies, the fight was a grimly sustained one. With vain heroism the Lancastrians, exalted by the Queen's presence, fought until they died. Somerset, taken prisoner, was beheaded the same evening—15 May 1464.

Margaret fled to the forest. In those days people spoke of Hexham forest as they spoke of Sherwood forest: the worst gangs of brigands had their lairs deep in the woods. One of these bands attacked the fugitives and stripped them of everything. In the course of sharing the loot the robbers fell to brawling, and Margaret, with her son's hand in hers seized her chance and ran away. When, exhausted, she was unable to run any further, she discovered that she had escaped from the robbers but was hopelessly lost.

The tale is that now night fell, a night of utter darkness without moon or stars, that the little prince, weeping, had at last fallen asleep; that the unhappy Queen passed hour after hour in those sombre woods in which every tree became a ghost and every bush a wild beast. She no longer knew hunger, exhaustion or despair, for terror in its most instinctive form, pure animal terror akin to madness, paralyzed all other feelings and gnawed at the very basis of reason. To a creature of the cities, or even of the villages, even the spectacle of death is as nothing by comparison with that primaeval darkness, haunted by every fabled horror, and infused with that mystery which is itself the very stuff of fear.

Then, the moon rose, and by its light the Queen saw a man coming towards her, a hairy, full-bearded man armed to the teeth, a robber. Now comes that scene which has become a legend and may be a myth. Margaret, true heroine, rises, holds out the boy prince towards the outlaw, and speaks: 'If it is gold you seek, I can give you none, for others before you have taken all I had. But if you have a heart which can be touched by pity, if once you had a mother who stooped over your cradle, I entrust this child to you. He is the son of your rightful King, heir to the crown of England. In saving him you will save your soul and your country. I place him under your protection.'

The man is taken aback: this woman's beauty, the charm of her voice, the little boy's grief, the idea of becoming the arbiter of so great a destiny, penetrates his rough hide. He takes the prince in his arms and leads the Queen to a refuge where none will find them. Later, he brings Brézé to them for the Seneschal, having escaped the . slaughter, has for several days been beating the country in search of the Queen and her son.

Such is the legend. Perhaps it is true.

This time the Red Rose seemed utterly destroyed, uprooted. Brézé persuaded the Queen to return to France. With an astounding mixture of cunning and courage he conveyed the proscribed Queen and the prince across a considerable extent of England and at last got them aboard a scarcely sea-worthy boat which put them ashore in Burgundian territory, somewhere in Flanders. Avoiding an ambush laid for them by English sent out from Calais, he got them to Bruges. From there Margaret, still unwilling or unable to give up the fight, sent to ask Philip the Good to receive her: in spite of old quarrels between their families she hoped to find the founder of the Order of the Golden Fleece more chivalrous and less cruelly usurious than Louis XI.

The meeting took place at Saint-Pol. The Duke was fatherly and compassionate, shedding tears as Margaret recounted her adventures (Like Louis XIV, Philip the Good could weep very easily). He showed the greatest concern and paid the Queen every respect. He gave orders that she was to be treated with all the honours due to royalty and he was the reverse of miserly with both guards and money. But when the Queen raised the political question, he showed marked reserve. Philip was then nearly seventy—a great age at that time, during the whole century only half a dozen out of scores of Valois and Plantagenet princes attained to sixty—his object now was to finish his reign in peace. He wanted to steer clear of such political and military adventures as his formidable son was only too apt to drag the Duchy into. In any case, the House of Burgundy had not yet made a clear choice between York and Lancaster; but if it came to that, its interest lay more with York than Lancaster. Burgundy was surely bound to support a young monarch greedy for military glory, feudal in his outlook and bound to the great feudal lords, rather than the unfortunate House of Lancaster represented by an invalid, a child and a discredited woman.

More magnanimous than Louis XI, Philip did not treat Margaret as an importunate beggar; but he drowned her pleas in a shower of gallant compliments and generosities.

He made use of his favourite diplomatic device, *fêtes*. He gave some magnificent feasts in several of his Flemish towns. And, following his example, the Duchess of Burgundy and the Count of Charolais made much of the Queen and her son, overwhelming them with kind attentions and presents and always yielding them the precedence due to their rank.

Margaret had not lost the privilege of being a winner and breaker of masculine hearts. The famous Burgundian chronicler Chastellain, moved by her beauty and touched by her misfortunes undertook the composition of a kind of philosophical treatise designed to console the illustrious exile.

In this curious work which is entitled *Temple of the*

*Ruin of Certain Noble Unfortunates* a vision appears to the author in his sleep, and 'came a voice to summon him' to rise and go to a certain cemetery. There appears to him 'the most doleful and discomforted Queen of England, leading her Lord, King Henry'. She passes beside the tomb of Boccaccio. The great story-teller rises from his grave and engages Margaret in a conversation which lasts for fifty chapters in which he recounts, by way of example, the misfortunes of numerous other princes, notably those of her uncle Charles VII and her father 'Regnier'. By way of conclusion the chronicler, 'shows this discomforted lady that there is nothing more propitious than, in true faith, to have recourse to God and to put all things in His hands'.

While the Burgundians tried in this fashion to distract the Queen's mind from her troubles, Louis XI and the Duke of Burgundy were agreeing together to treat with her enemies. When his plan had miscarried, Louis had immediately approached Warwick. He knew that the great feudal lords were ready to league themselves together against him, and he regarded peace with England as imperatively necessary. Philip the Good was not willing that any such peace be concluded excepting under his personal supervision. He imposed himself on France and England as mediator. A conference was held at Hesdin, presided over by the Grand Duke of the West. It would seem to have been dangerous for Louis to leave his '*bel oncle*' to manage these delicate negotiations. But on that side also the royal fox had made plans to cover his own interests.

The Croys, the favourites who completely ruled Philip the Good, knew that they were loathed by the Duchess and her son. When the knell tolled for the old prince they knew that it would be tolling for them likewise. So, wishing to make provision for their retreat when it became necessary, they had secretly taken service with the King.

By their means Louis XI had all the threads of Burgundian policy in his hands: the Croys were even able, in due course, to persuade their aged master to sell Louis those guardians of the Duchy and mortgages on France, the Somme towns. Louis also, as we have seen, had the threads of Yorkist policy in his hands by means of his agent Warwick. So that he could await the decision of the Hesdin plenipotentiaries without anxiety; it was Louis who pulled the strings.

The Truce between England and France was signed on 27 October 1463. In order to seal it, and at the same time to have the means of influencing Edward's mind, Louis stipulated that the young King Edward must marry the lady Bonne of Savoy, the Queen of France's sister. Warwick accepted this clause but had no intention of implementing it: he was reserving the Queen's crown of England for his own daughter, Isabel Neville.

So, then, Margaret found herself repudiated not only by France but by Burgundy. Less even than before could she count on her own people. John of Calabria returned to France, having once again lost Italy. Brézé managed to persuade his lady to resign herself to defeat, at least for the time being; to wait for better things and for the Prince of Wales to reach young manhood. Margaret accordingly asked her father to ensure her at least the means of a decent livelihood. After numerous tiresome difficulties, due to the confused state of his finances, the old King granted her the castle of Koeur near Verdun which he had retained when, at the death of Isabel of Lorraine, he had had to hand over the whole Duchy to John of Calabria. He also allowed her a modest pension of 2,000 *livres*.

Thenceforth, Margaret devoted herself solely to the education of the Prince of Wales. The wise Fortescue, Henry VI's old preceptor, had come to join her. He undertook to furnish the boy's mind, as he had furnished his father's, surrounding his pupil with the best masters, and developing his body by the practice of even the most dangerous forms of exercise.

In this almost unknown retreat, then, it seemed that the poor Queen might at last enjoy a respite. But the Furies had by no means done with her yet. And first they deprived her of Brézé.

When the Seneschal returned with the Queen, Louis XI, about to open his campaign against the great feudal lords, and being short of reliable officers, had opened his arms to his father's old minister. He overwhelmed him with favours, and married Brézé's son to an illegitimate daughter of Charles VII and Agnes Sorel. Brézé did not try to avoid his duty, although he went to it without much enthusiasm. Margaret could not forgive the King his alliance with the Yorkists, and doubtless it was she who persuaded her friend not to show the door to emissaries sent by the Duke of Berry, Louis' brother and enemy, and the Count of Charolais.

Meanwhile, things began to move swiftly as Louis started his war on the barons. Victorious in the south, he had to return by forced marches to Paris, for there was a danger that the Burgundians and Bretons would get there first. Numerous informers were advising him not to trust Brézé. Louis, intending to ensure Brézé's loyalty by giving him the post of honour and so appealing to his pride, entrusted him with the vanguard. But the Count's attitude remained enigmatical.

The two armies met at Montlhèry. There the King received confirmation that the Seneschal had received emissaries from Berry and Charolais; and it was reported that he had uttered some very dangerous words, saying that he would place the adversaries 'so close to one another that he would be a very clever man who could disentangle them'. Louis sent for his general and asked him if he had really given his signature to the rebels. Brézé, unfortunately and inexpediently a wit, could not resist answering with a

witticism: *'Ils ont l'escrit, le corps vous restera.'** He had
damned himself. At the first clash between the leading
troops on both sides, Brézé fell mortally wounded. Was
he struck down by an enemy soldier or by one of the
King's agents? That will never be known.

While Margaret was still mourning her friend with
tears, terrible news of her husband reached her. In the
security of Berwick castle guarded by a Scottish garrison,
Henry seemed safe enough. He had been living there for
two years in apparent tranquillity.

One day, however, the poor King felt a strong home-
sickness for his own country, his own house, his own
family. With the cunning of a sleep-walker he evaded the
vigilance of his guards and escaped. Ah, what happiness
to feel the earth of England under one's feet, to walk at
liberty, far from those grim walls and watchful sentries.
It was the end of spring and bright sunshine warmed all
things into friendliness. The King errant wandered at
random, from village to village, sharing the black bread
of the peasants, and sleeping under their thatch. And this
contact with the simple life of the country people delighted
him: should not this learning to know his subjects, living
their life, be a King's foremost task? He was asked his
name and did not conceal it. Had not all men a soul like
his own? He had forgotten his enemies.

The rumour of his presence in the countryside passed
from mouth to ear, mouth to ear. It reached the ear of a
Yorkist captain who sought out the King, captured him
without difficulty, and handed him over to Warwick.

Thereupon the Yorkists were guilty of an act of hideous
dastardliness, an act which dishonours their name in
history much more certainly than their worst massacres.
Tied to the saddle of his horse, Henry the Saintly was

* As if to say, 'They have the shadow, the substance will be yours.' The
joke is untranslateable, depending on the play between *escrit* (writing) and
*esprit*.

paraded through the streets of London like the vilest malefactor exposed in the stocks. The scum of the city, the sweepings of the docks and suburbs, skilfully mustered and roused, booed and insulted him, flung filth in his face, while Warwick proclaimed him an ignominious usurper, and did not forget the Queen, the abominated Frenchwoman, described as 'that ribald creature, shameless with her body'.

After several hours of this torture Warwick imprisoned Henry in the Tower. The Yorkists' intention was to present the Lancasters as shamed and degraded before the world. In the event they rehabilitated them, wiping out the memory of their shortcomings. For among all the cruel, violent men and woman—not excepting Margaret herself—who did each other to death in the course of that atrocious war, Henry, and only Henry, was constant in decent humanity, clement and generous. To him alone was it given to endure martyrdom and by his martyrdom to redeem something of the vileness, something of the bloodshed.

# The King Maker

The White Rose victory was complete. Just as the French Revolution was for a long time able to withstand economic storms by the expedient of selling off national assets, so the power of the House of York was firmly based on the new distribution of the national lands. The territorial domains of the opposition, and even of those families which remained lukewarm or uncommitted, were confiscated and handed over to loyal Yorkists. Added to which there was much creating of new titles. Two thirds of the Lords were thus persuaded to defend Edward's throne as if it were their own property.

As for Edward himself, like a later, 'constitutional' monarch, he reigned but did not rule. This marvellously gifted young prince, so brave and skilful in battle, was ruined by his own personal beauty. Accustomed to adoration, he was much too inclined to despise virtues which his charm seemed to make unnecessary—at least to him. And becoming used to satisfying all his desires and wishes immediately, this English Adonis became, little by little, their slave.

Having a fair share of his family's evil disposition, the radiant adolescent was transformed into an arid-hearted princeling, ill-natured, sensual and self-indulgent, blindly submissive to the demands of his own pleasure-seeking, and quite ready to break any man who thwarted his whims. All this was by no means displeasing to Warwick, who could be sure that the realities of power would never be taken from him by a King absorbed in the pleasures of the table, hunting and debauchery.

The Earl—he was already being called the King Maker—was now at the zenith of his power. His latest victories had won him more spoils and offices and the people idolized him for his ostentatious magnificence and his open-handed charities. Warwick held the Clergy in his hand through his brother, the Archbishop of York; the nobility through his other brother Montagu, and a host of other lords who had hitched their wagon to his star; the soldiers, because of his standing as a soldier, his military victories; the navy because he was their Admiral; the corsairs by means of his traffic in contraband; and a whole horde of ruffians and adventurers by means of subsidies and complicities. His court eclipsed many a sovereign's and it was said of him that he daily fed hordes of followers at his tables.

There was only one cloud between him and Edward: he wanted to make a Queen of England out of his daughter, Elizabeth Neville, at that time fourteen years of age. The King was unwilling to marry the girl, considering her too young. Apart from that there was complete harmony between them; a harmony which was very soon to be destroyed by a woman.

Elizabeth Woodville was the daughter of Jacqueline of Luxembourg who had been married to the Duke of Bedford, Henry V's brother, and after the Duke's death had married one of his former 'domestics', Sir Richard Woodville. Elizabeth was a dazzling beauty from her cradle. She was taken to Court where Margaret took a fancy to her and made her one of her ladies-in-waiting. There were many suitors for the hand of this ravishing creature, the Queen's favourite, the lucky man being Lord

John Grey, later Lord Ferrers, a convinced Lancastrian; he was killed at the second battle of St Albans.

Widowed and ruined, and with the Queen, her patroness, in flight, Elizabeth took her two children and sought refuge with her family in Grafton Castle. For some years she led a straitened and obscure life there, but always determined to escape from it. One day she heard that the King was hunting in a nearby forest. She hurried there, placed herself at a crossroads, and when the King appeared, threw herself at his feet and implored him to restore her children's lands to them. Edward looked long and hard at the lovely young widow—and the future of England was changed.

Although she was the mother of a family, her elder child being about seven years old, Edward clearly and immediately showed that he was madly in love with her, and insisted that she return with him to London. She agreed to do so, but held the bait well out of reach, making much of her virtue, which made the King more amorous than ever. He secretly married her on 1 May 1464. Always incapable of self-control, Edward did not hesitate to stake his throne, indifferent to the Archbishop of York's cry that if he insisted on marrying the woman it would cost the lives of 10,000 men. Elizabeth Woodville donned the crown of her former patroness, and became England's Queen.

Great was the rage of Warwick and his party. The most they could hope or the least expect was that this scheming hussy would do everything in her power to get herself forgiven for her shocking elevation. They could hardly have been more completely mistaken.

Elizabeth had a numerous family—father, brothers, a swarm of cousins, all as ambitious as they were grasping. About them revolved a coterie of hangers-on all bent on making something for themselves out of Elizabeth's good fortune. The new Queen persuaded her husband that he

would never rule as well as reign while he remained at
Warwick's mercy. Who knew but that one day the King
Maker might not take it into his head to wear the crown
himself? To avoid this danger, let Edward create a
following of men dependent for their preferment not on the
Earl but on the King himself, and bind to himself families
able and willing to defend him against all comers. Edward
listened and was persuaded.

There are few examples in history of such a place-hunter's
goldrush that followed. Not a vacant place or property,
not an abbey, not an heiress escaped in the great gathering
in of every kind of benefice organized by the Queen's
relations and their friends. Titles, lands, jobs and concessions rained down on their heads. Sir Richard Woodville,
created Earl Rivers, was given a seat in the Council, as
was his kinsman Lord Hastings. But they were an insatiable crew; to get more and still more they did not shrink
from extortion, menaces and blackmail; the venerable and
octogenarian Duchess of Norfolk was forced into marriage
with a Court loafer of twenty, so that he could come into
her property.

Having taken that road, the King was under the necessity of ensuring solid support for himself abroad. And
since Warwick was still engaged in his obscure transactions with Louis XI, Edward turned to the Duke of
Burgundy.

Philip the Good had just died on 15 June 1467 and his
son Charles was now in sole control of his people's
destiny, a man driven by fierce ambition, a man without
insight or foresight, who was to take only ten years to
bring his brilliant empire to ruin. At the height of his
struggle with France, nothing could have been more to
the point at this moment than an English alliance. He
responded to Edward's advances by asking for the hand
of Edward's sister, Margaret of York.

In July 1468 the princess landed in Flanders where the

wedding was celebrated near Bruges on 3 July 1468 with great splendour. It was a grim union, this marriage between two blood-drenched houses, each equally near to the term of its greatness, each stamped with fate's last verdict. During the wedding night the nuptial bed caught fire, which was widely taken to be a presage of great calamities. The young Duchess, however, had she but known it, might have thanked Heaven for her lot; out of the sixteen princes and princesses of her immediate family she was one of only two to die a natural death, the other being her niece Elizabeth of York, Henry VII's wife.

Warwick felt the ground shifting beneath his feet. He was no longer the great dispenser of favours. The King was making and signing treaties on his own account. It would not be long before the Nevilles were no longer the greatest and richest family in England. The Earl made up his mind to put a prompt stop to such abuses. But to frighten Edward he needed a prince of Edward's own blood.

Richard of York had had five children by Cecily Neville; one daughter, the Duchess of Burgundy—and four sons. The eldest was King Edward, the second, Edmund, had been killed by Clifford at Wakefield; the third, George, Duke of Clarence was a fat young man of twenty, indolent, sensual and self-indulgent, without a spark of fire and easily led; the fourth and youngest, Richard, Duke of Gloucester was, of course, Richard III, hunchback and devil, or straightbacked and an angel according to which side one takes in the controversy about his nature and conduct.

The Earl of Warwick chose Clarence and betrothed him to his own daughter Isabel. Edward, of course, strongly opposed the marriage which was obviously full of danger for himself; but to no purpose. The King Maker took the young couple to Calais, where he was the sole master under God, and, on 11 July 1469, had them married.

The struggle between the King and the Earl now began. As Edward, his will and spirit stiffened by his wife's influence, showed no sign of amendment, Warwick took a high-handed line. One morning in September, the King woke with a start to find his bedroom invaded by a delegation of Yorkist lords led by the Archbishop of Canterbury. Down on one knee, the Archbishop begged his gracious master to rise and dress himself and to go with them without raising an outcry, which could only endanger his life. Edward complied, and was conveyed under a strong escort to Middleham Castle, one of Warwick's estates.

Was Clarence now to occupy the throne? Charles the Bold of Burgundy, for one, was against it. He sent a letter written in ringing terms to Parliament saying that in marrying Margaret of York he had allied himself to England in the person of her King. He would consider any offence done to that prince as a personal insult to himself; and Edward's deposition as a *casus belli*. One consequence would be closure of the Flemish ports to English products for as long as the rightful king was not restored to power. Now that simple declaration of intent was worth a dozen armies: powerful though Warwick might be, he did not weigh one ounce against the kingdom's commercial interests. Moreover at that particular moment in time Charles the Bold was the most feared and respected monarch in Europe; he had just wrung the Treaty of Péronne out of Louis XI; and the recent massacres of Dinan and Liège had given him a fearsome repute. In short, Warwick was forced to give way and, loudly protesting his loyalty, to bring his prisoner back to London. He had, he said, no quarrel with the King, but only with the King's evil councillors. Nevertheless, relations between the two men became impossibly strained. And fearful of being assassinated, the Earl went back to Calais, taking Clarence with him.

When it became known that Warwick was leaving the

kingdom, something very like a panic spread through the multitude of people accustomed to gravitate round him, and a whole horde of Lords, soldiers, and adventurers hastened to join him. Unfortunately, the spectacle of this motley army alarmed the Captain of Calais who shut the town gates in his master's face. Warwick had no alternative but to ask Louis XI for asylum.

He could not have arrived at a better moment.

France seemed ready to topple and crash again into the ruinous state in which Joan of Arc had found it. The Treaty of Péronne seemed quite likely to wipe out the results of forty years of victories and hard work. Like monstrous hydra, the great feudatories encircled the realm in a deadly embrace: the enormous Duchy of Guyenne, created as an apanage for the King's brother, threatened the kingdom from the south-west; Burgundy, once again mistress of the Somme towns, was in a position to strangle France to death. There was a plan to wed Charles of Guyenne to Marie of Burgundy, to create for the young prince's benefit a formidable principality which might easily crush Louis XI between north and south. And both the Breton and Savoyard dukes expected their share of the quarry.

The King had but few friends: the officer commanding his army, the Constable de Saint-Pol, and a few men bought with favour piled on favour, like the Duke of Nemours. His beloved minister, la Balue, was openly betraying him. Like John the Good at Poitiers, he had to guard himself on both right and left. If, in addition to all this, he had to face an English invasion—and how could Edward IV refuse that help to his brother-in-law after the last service Charles had done him?—then the prodigious progress accomplished during the reign of Charles VII would be wiped out and France would relapse, be back again where she was in 1420 at the time of the Treaty of Troyes. Worse, perhaps, she might be reduced to the

Merovingian dismemberment, become again Neustria and
Austrasia.

Louis must, therefore, cast a firebrand into England at
the first possible moment: ablaze at home, she would be
in no case to intervene abroad. Thus in June 1470 Louis
welcomed his dear Warwick like a Messiah; the two
business partners examined the situation coldly and soon
came to the conclusion that the weak and vacillating
Clarence would be a most inadequate hero. To be really
significant any new revolution in England must begin by
raising the Lancastrian standard.

It was at this juncture that the King remembered his
'*belle cousine*' who, for five years, had been vegetating in
Koeur Castle. He sent to ask her to come and confer
with him.

Was Margaret to save France once again, then? Certainly it was to that end that the crafty royal politician had
made up his mind to bring about the most improbable of
alliances—an alliance between Lancaster and Warwick.

For an observer of men as clever as Louis XI, a man so
skilful in making use of the waywardness of the human
heart, it must have been an intellectual pleasure of the
highest order to be present at the duel between two people
so utterly different from each other that they were at
opposite ends of the human spectrum. Margaret, very
much a woman despite her physical heroism, ruled by her
feelings and her impulses, believing in love and hate, and
in the logic and continuity of those passions. Warwick,
the slave of personal interests, incapable of either hating
or serving by any rule but that of expediency, perfectly
ready to shatter his own idols, the moment they ceased to
serve his ambitions.

The Earl had been one of the first to accuse the Queen
of betraying England to France, and to blame her for the

disasters in Normandy and Guyenne, and for Talbot's death, sparing her nothing in his determination to make her, in the people's eyes, a figure of horror and shame. He had asked Parliament to declare that 'the Frenchwoman's' rule had been 'great injustice and oppression'; had denounced the abominable immorality of this new Messalina in the House of Lords; and had proclaimed her son a bastard. Physically and morally he had hounded her with a rage which nothing in her life could excuse; and pilloried her invalid husband, exposing him to the outrages of the rabble. Yet now, as if it were the most natural thing in the world, he was offering his sword and swearing to defend her cause to the death.

Margaret could not bring herself to conceive of such utter unawareness or such total cynicism. But yielding at last to the urgings and objurgations of the King, she agreed to meet the Earl and a formal reconciliation was arranged, to be staged on 22 July 1470. Yet the mere sight of her enemy made her forget any promises of moderation which she had made. She overwhelmed Warwick with curses, called him a faithless lackey, a slanderer and a coward. The Kingmaker bore the storm of abuse with humility, with a countenance so perfectly what it ought to be that Louis XI was delighted with him.

When, running out of breath or imprecations, the Queen fell silent, Warwick protested his repentance and his loyalty at considerable length, and then got down to business, showed her Edward as isolated, despised, even in the midst of the dishonoured and discredited Rivers coterie. If he, Warwick, proclaimed himself Henry VI's champion, then a union between the two Roses would be accomplished amid general rejoicing. There would not even be any fighting: deprived of its props, Edward's throne would collapse pitifully. And remember that even Clarence, his own brother, would be marching against him.

Louis strongly supported these reasons, displaying all

the wheedling charm which he could, on occasion and when he had to, call up. He promised unqualified and unconditional support—men, money, all they needed. But all these arguments could not overcome Margaret's repugnance, her instinctive revulsion from both men. Heroic, downright, she had in her nothing of the statesman, and persisted in wanting men to be what they should be, and not as circumstances had made them.

Informed of the danger which threatened him, Edward IV tried to ward it off. He sent to the Queen proposing a pact of reconciliation: if the Prince of Wales would marry his daughter Elizabeth—a child of three or four at the time—he would recognize the Prince as his heir.

Alarmed at the possibility of an accommodation of which he would have been the first victim, Louis XI did all in his power to turn Margaret away from the idea. And in point of fact it would have been an arrangement which arranged nothing: Elizabeth Woodville had just born a son—the future Edward V, one of the princes in the tower —and moreover the King's brothers, particularly Gloucester, would never have subscribed to such a treaty.

Poor Margaret became a prey to a harrowing dilemma involving her conscience as a mother. For her own part she would not have hesitated to refuse an alliance with Warwick. But had she the right to deny her son one more chance? After a painful struggle with herself, maternal feelings overcame instinctive revulsion. The Queen sacrificed her hatred and her womanly pride to her son, and forgave Warwick. But that was not enough for Louis: he wanted a guarantee of the alliance from which he expected the security of France from invasion. Warwick had hoped and expected that his eldest daughter would be Queen of England, and had been disappointed of his expectation; well, never mind, they would place the crown in question on the brow of his second daughter, the charming Anne Neville.

Margaret drew back at that: that cup was really too bitter. Was she to give her son, by way of father-in-law, a man who had risen in Parliament to call him a bastard? God himself could not bless so monstrous a union. Despite all his craft the King might have failed at this point, had he not found an ally in the young prince himself. Edward of Lancaster was near the end of his sixteenth year: physically and intellectually precocious, he was likeable, even charming, courageous and burning with determination to reconquer his birthright, and above all to get away from the tedious and shabby life which he and his mother led at Koeur Castle. He saw Anne, a pretty, gentle girl of fourteen; and shortly announced that he was in love with her. Attacked on all sides, her heart torn, the Queen gave way.

The Earl of Warwick swore on the cross to serve the House of Lancaster. And King Louis of France undertook to spare nothing in order to ensure the triumph of their cause.

The wedding was celebrated at Amboise in August 1470, with truly royal splendour. All the princes of the Houses of France and Anjou were present, and also the Duke of Clarence who was said to have come over to the Red Rose in exchange for a non-existent apanage.

Louis XI was making himself responsible for Margaret's expenses, and subsidising the Prince and his young wife. The books of Jean Briconnet, Receiver of Finances, contain the entry: 'My Lady the Queen of England, for her expenses, of the Prince of Wales, her son, of my Lady Anne, daughter of M. de Warwick and wife of the said prince, in the months of August, September and October, 1470, 2,550 *livres*, and in the months of November and December, for the furnishing of their silver ware, 2,831 *livres* and 1,000 *livres* for their pleasures.' Margaret was treated as a reigning sovereign; she was overwhelmed with honours; and she was on the eve of her revenge and restoration. Yet she could not feel happy. She was wondering whether this 'unnatural' wedding was not tempting fate, and tortured by premonitory anguish, seemed already to see the wedding feast torches transformed into funeral candles.

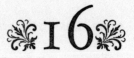

# The Last Battle

Nature the ironist had given Henry VI the soul of a monk or a martyr: this is a game which she seems, indeed, to take pleasure in as great dynasties decline and draw towards their end. Louis XVI was to show himself a hundred times more regal and more master of his rôle as a prisoner in the Temple, than at Versailles. Thus too, the son of Henry V, so very inadequate on the throne, showed the full measure of his touching genius only in the Tower of London.

In that prison, where his warders deprived him of the most elementary attentions, his mystical spirit, refined and fortified by suffering, attained the remote summits of the mystery. The very few people who were admitted to his presence were confounded by his nobility and by his serenity. The captive King divided his mind, his soul, into two: became, in some sort, his own medium. It is said that one day he called his guards and urged them to hasten down to the Thames where a woman was trying to drown herself and her child. The King was obeyed, and the despairing woman was found and saved. Sick people sought, as a special favour, the right to be touched by the healing hand of this seer.* And so

* *Translator's Note:* The power to cure by touch was not, as Monsieur Erlanger implies in this passage, peculiarly Henry's, but was an attribute

great was their trust in his powers that several were cured.

Should we do well to feel sorry for Henry during the years of his captivity? Despite the grief which he experienced at being cut off from his wife and his son, those may have been the years during which he felt most nearly himself. He had scratched on the wall of his room in the Tower the words 'royalty is only care'. Freed from the terrible questions of conscience propounded by the exercise of power, and with the strict, harsh rules imposed by his gaolers taking the place of monastic rules, Henry lived as his tastes would have him live, in an ascetic tranquillity, already half-dead, and very close to his God.

We may, then, rather begin to be sorry for him from that day in September when the corridors of the ancient keep were suddenly filled with the clamour of voices and the clash of weapons; when the door of the room burst open and the most implacable of his enemies appeared. Had Warwick come at last to complete his crime? Henry rose to his feet, ready to appear before his Maker and already—if we know him—forgiving his murderers. But then the Earl fell at his prisoner's feet, appealed to his clemency, and proclaimed him sole master and lord of all England; and meanwhile all present were bursting into cries of 'Long live Henry, Henry the Saint!'

Then the King realized that Heaven was calling upon him to make a sacrifice even more painful than that of life itself; and submissive as always to the will of God, he accepted his crown of thorns with a sigh.

A barber was summoned to cut his hair and shave him; he was dressed in royal clothes and lifted on to a palfrey

of regality. In this case, however, the fact that persons suffering from the 'King's Evil' (probably a psychosomatic skin disease) sought Henry's touch does mean that the people regarded Henry as their rightful King, for obviously a usurper would not be thought to possess this power which came from God. E.H.

and paraded through London, following much the same route as his calvary of six years ago when the mob spat on him and threw filth at him. And as on that occasion an excited, clamorous crowd pressed round him—only this time it was a clamour of love and passionate veneration.

Warwick had sailed for England before the last echoes of the great wedding feast had faded away. The moment he set foot on land his family, his hangers-on, his creditors and his ruffians came running and bleating about him like a strayed flock finding its lost shepherd. Close to 60,000 men marched with him on his road to London. Edward mustered his partisans and went out to meet the rebels. But as soon as the two armies made contact near Nottingham all the Yorkists promptly deserted Edward and went over to Warwick. Left almost alone the King was forced to seek safety in flight, which he was in such a violent hurry to do that he did not even find time to warn his wife, leaving her and her children in the victor's hands. Two months later Louis XI declared war on the Duke of Burgundy.

O miraculous virtue of the *coup d'etat*! The English nation suddenly found itself Lancastrian again. But the credit for this, if credit there be, was certainly not the nation's: Henry's restoration was the work of Edward's former friends. Which fact meant, of course, that their new estates were safe: and they were right to think so, for indeed no change whatever was made in the former Yorkist share-out of landed property. But the guarantee was a short-term one and might turn into a threat at any time. Meanwhile, however, everyone was ready to worship at the altar of the saint on the throne. Daily, children were brought to him for his blessing. The Earl of Pembroke, Owen Tudor's second son, brought him his young nephew, Henry of Richmond, who was then fifteen years of age; there is some story that Henry VI recognized that the boy would someday reign.

Fifteen years later this boy, then so remote from the throne, became Henry VII.

Meanwhile, Margaret and her son were waiting on the coast of Normandy to enjoy their share of these transports of loyalty. It had been agreed that after Warwick's departure the Queen should remain in France, to join the Earl with more recruits as soon as success was assured. Success was now assured; but contrary winds prevented the royal family from sailing for several months.

It was almost as if the winds were obeying Louis of France. Far from sure of his cousin and deeply distrustful of her hot-headed impulsiveness, the King was anxious to leave Warwick time to get his rule firmly established before encumbering him with that turbulent woman. And Margaret was in a mood of profound gloom, her mind a prey to yet more causes for grieving.

On 16 December 1470 John of Calabria had died suddenly in Catalonia where he was fighting for the crown of Aragon. With him vanished all the hopes of the House of Anjou. His brother-in-law, Ferry de Vaudemont had died shortly before him; and in both cases there was suspicion—and traces—of poisoning. The Queen began to feel that she and all those connected with her were the playthings of a malignant fate.

Edward, meanwhile, had landed in Holland in territory which was a part of Duke Charles the Bold's estates, and he hastened to his brother-in-law's court to ask for aid and protection. Great and terrible was the Burgundian's rage at seeing all his plans set at nought. Louis had certainly won the first round; so be it, but he should not win the second. As a result of that resolution, Edward was back in England by 10 March 1471, landing at the small port of Ravenspur with a powerful escort provided and paid for by his ally. He marched at once, not on London, however, but to York. What was he claiming? The throne again? Not at all. He respected Parliament's decision, making way for Henry since the nation had, for the second time, elected the Lancastrian. All he was reclaiming was his own, his Duchy of York. Just as, in 1399, Henry Bolingbroke, the future Henry IV had raised his standard against Richard II to recover, as he declared, the patrimony of the House of Lancaster.

It was a clever pretext, well calculated to appeal to English hearts. In England birthright is something sacred; or was. It would have been unthinkable to prevent a son from fighting for what had been his father's and his ancestors?

So this magical formula smoothed Edward's way for him. And he had another talisman which was of service to him: his face. At every great house where he halted and asked for hospitality, he won the men over by his filial argument—that he was entitled to his birthright; and he won over the women by his glances and sighs; all of them were out of their senses about this prince as beautiful as Antinoüs and as brave as a Knight of the Round Table. They emptied their purses into his hands: Michelet tells the story of an old woman from whom he asked ten marks; 'For that face,' she said, 'you shall have twenty'. And the women urged their fathers, husbands, brothers to take up the defence of so noble a cause as Edward's. Promises did the rest, and quite soon Edward had an army and a war chest. At that point he gave up talking about his Duchy and marched on London.

When the news of Edward's march reached Margaret on the other side of the Channel, her old fighting instincts were revived. Neither her age—she was forty—nor seven years of domestic, almost housewifely existence, had quite suppressed her taste for warlike excitements, nor modified her impatience to meet her enemies face to face. Her son shared her spirited feelings. Disdaining the sailors' fears and warnings, gloomy prognostications, the bad auguries of the astrologers and Louis XI's prudent advice, the Queen and the Prince set sail with their little army. The young Princess of Wales accompanied her husband.

So rough was the weather which they met with that the ships took a fortnight to beat across the Channel. But they dropped anchor at last in Weymouth harbour on 13 April 1471, the eve of Easter. Violent squalls, fog, snow and unseasonable cold greeted Margaret just as they had done twenty-six years earlier when she first set foot in this hostile land. Once again the very spirits of the air seemed bent on keeping her away from the fate in store for her. But such Fates rule even the very gods.

The Queen was expecting a message from Warwick before she could follow him. But on the day following the landing at Weymouth the Kingmaker was otherwise engaged—in the battle of Barnet against Edward IV.

At the very first onset the Duke of Clarence went over to the White Rose and Lord Montagu, Warwick's own brother, started haranguing the troops in favour of their master, Edward. The Great Earl saw fate's balance swinging against him. With a blow of his sword one of his men split Montagu's skull while he, himself, repeating the gesture he had made at Towton, killed his horse and swore to vanquish or to die on the field.

As at Towton, there was darkness at noon, a twilight of fog and rain. Despite their loyalty to their leader, it was not without some hesitation that Warwick's soldiers fought against a prince for whom their elder brothers had shed oceans of blood. Moreover, they had a stroke of sheer bad luck when, misled by the bad light, two companies of the Red Rose charged each other. And again, Fortune, following a fashion set by the English ladies, threw her kerchief to the handsomer of the two sovereigns. The Lancastrians were crushed. And, perhaps for the first time in his life, the Kingmaker honoured an oath: for he lay among the dead.

London, worshipping, or at least accepting, success like the Rome of Marius and Sulla, acclaimed the victor. And back went Henry VI to his cell in the Tower.

Margaret was shattered by the news of this disaster. For a brief while she gave way to a prophetic terror and in spite of her son's protests gave orders to return to France. But at the critical moment reinforcements began to arrive.

The knights of the Red Rose, the real loyalists, had, until that moment, made no move to help: their hatred or distrust of Warwick was too strong. But as soon as they heard that the Queen herself was in England, they flocked to her standard. They were led by Edmund Beaufort, now fourth Duke Somerset, and his brother John. Among them was a somewhat equivocal personage, Lord John Wenlock, formerly Margaret's Chamberlain, whose shufflings and shuttlings between the two sides were by now almost past counting. But, in the circumstances, the Lancastrians were in no position to be too particular.

All of them were young men, some of them scarcely more than twenty: they were of the third generation to be flung as sacrificial victims to this patricidal warfare. Without hesitation, animated by a serene heroism, they came to fill the places of fathers who had fallen at Towton or Hexham, of grandfathers who had died at St Albans. With all the fervour of their youth, they were eager for battle. They assured the Queen that the defeat and death of Warwick and his people should be considered as a public benefit. What King could have pretended that he was indeed the ruler, in the shade of that all-devouring giant? It was proper, then, to praise God for the loss of so terrible an ally and seize the chance to strike at the White Rose now crippled by a Pyrrhic victory. Besides, the Tudors were busy raising in Wales an army which would make the Red Rose numerically equal to their adversaries.

The young prince eagerly urged and supported this opinion and the Queen gave way. But the splendid enthusiasm of the past was gone, overlaid by sombre presentiments.

The Lancastrians wanted to begin by making a junction with the Tudors. To do so they had to cross the Severn. Thrown back at Gloucester by a Yorkist garrison, they had to move up river by forced marches to the other bridge at Tewkesbury. Unfortunately Edward had foreseen this and had marched there even faster: encamped beside the river, he was waiting for his enemies.

On that day—4 May 1471—the depression of sudden heat was added to the troubles of soldiers already exhausted by hard marching. Following the advice of a majority of her officers, the Queen decided to refuse battle. But it was written that the Somerset family was to be the bane of the Lancasters to the very last: with extraordinary violence, the Duke protested, guaranteed the ardour of his troops, argued that a retreat would demoralize them and would, indeed, give the usurper the chance to consolidate his position. Supported by the Prince of Wales, eager to win his spurs, Somerset at last wrung from the Queen the order to offer battle.

Each side knew that it was now a case of all or nothing, that the future was staked on the coming battle, and that the vanquished, even those who came whole out of the fight, would that night sup with Pluto. The two Somersets were as obstinate in the fight as they were brave. John Beaufort, mortally wounded, was not long in joining his kinsmen who had died in the same cause. Stricken with grief, the Duke his brother now found Lord John Wenlock's companies halting, for no reason, their part of a movement in a manoeuvre which had been started. Flinging himself at that agile turncoat, he cut him down with his own hand. But this act, instead of inspiring the men with fresh courage, only spread uncertainty and disorder.

Soon the Queen, who was following the progress of the battle in all its phases, saw her battalions open, break; saw

Somerset taken prisoner, then the Prince of Wales un-horsed and captured. At that she became again the warrior Queen, cried out for a horse, a sword that she, too, might die as a soldier. With all her strength she fought against her servants who were trying to drag her away to safety, struggled to fight her way on to the field of battle now covered with the dead. In this crisis, this hysteria, the Yorkists came upon the scene. Unconscious she was thrown into a cart and, with her daughter-in-law, taken to a nearby convent and there imprisoned.

Victorious, but still thirsting for blood, Edward ordered the immediate execution of Somerset and the other prisoners, excepting the Prince of Wales.

A few days later, seated on his throne and surrounded by his Lords, he had his young rival brought before him. Neither the boy's youthful beauty, nor his dignity, nor his bravery, nor the magnificent eyes of the seventeen-year-old prince, eyes still innocent of life's realities, softened the fierce hearts of his enemies. The King asked him with what object he was come in arms against his rightful lord. Proud of answering his enemy like a hero of antiquity, the youth replied,

'To avenge my father and to recover my birthright.'

With his iron-studded gauntlet Edward struck him in the face; and the pack hurled themselves on the prey thus thrown to them. Stabbed and hacked by their daggers, the boy died without a single word or cry of pain.

On the following day, 11 May 1471, Margaret, still ignorant of this tragedy and ready to fight for her son's life with the ferocity of a lioness defending her young, was taken from her convent cell to appear in her turn before the King. On the way the captain of the escort gave him-self the pleasure of telling her what had happened to the Prince. Under that terrible blow her reason deserted her and the creature who confronted her child's murderer was a Niobe, possessed by the rage of the Furies. She overwhelmed Edward with insults and curses, hoping to provoke him into killing her likewise. But that bitter satisfaction was denied her. Either as an exercise in refined cruelty, or because he was ashamed to put a woman to death, or because he secretly admired her, the King shrank from committing yet another such crime. He took Margaret to London where she, too, was thrown into the Tower but was not allowed the consolation of seeing her husband. The unhappy woman believed that she had now drained the bitter cup, that nothing worse could possibly happen to her. She was mistaken.

The murder of Henry VI in the Tower during the night of 22/23 May 1471 has been attributed to Richard Plantagenet, Edward's brother, the future Richard III. But so, also, was the murder of Edward, Prince of Wales, after Tewkesbury, which we have attributed, following one set of accounts, to the King who, according to another account, was not personally involved or responsible. Richard has been made the scapegoat for all the Yorkist crimes by Lancastrian and Tudor historians: it is *possible* that he was a hunchback; but his two contemporary portraits show no sign of it, nor do contemporary descriptions mention it; it is *possible* that he was a black-hearted villain—but the weight of evidence is against his guilt for either Edward of Lancaster's death, or that of King Henry. The probability is that Richard was neither more nor less ruthless than the other grandees of his time, than his brother Edward, for example. The worth of the opinions concerning him published by Tudor apologists after his death can be judged by the story that even when he was a youth his breath blown upon a flower would make it wilt and fade. Much of the quite incredible legend of Richard's wickedness is, of course, due to Shakespeare; and it was expedient for Shakespeare to keep the matter of his plays pleasing to the Tudors.

Be that as it may, Henry VI was murdered in the Tower

and it is as difficult to believe that this crime was committed without Edward's connivance as that Richard stabbed the King with his own hand. It is said that the King was sleeping when his murderer entered his cell; and that he did not move, nor make any resistance to the assassin's dagger. Perhaps he had been forewarned by one of those messages which are received by holy simpletons. There is an ancient belief that God grants his elect the blessing of seeing, at their last moment of life, a vision of their dearest love or the supreme hope of their days. It may be that at the instant of quitting an atrocious world, Henry the Saint saw stooping over him the form of the young princess who had long ago come to him out of Anjou to bring him happiness, martyrdom and death.

# Between Sunset and Dawn

On 25 August 1475 the inhabitants of the little town of Picquigny in Normandy were regaled with a spectacle worthy to be put on canvas by a historical painter with a sense of humour.

On one hand was one of the most magnificent armies ever to appear, until that date, on the Continent, 15,000 knights and 14,000 archers drawn up in battle array, with gorgeous caparisons, damascened armour and glittering lances. On the other about 1,000 men-at-arms under the lilies of France. Between these two, the Seine and a bridge, but a bridge transformed into a cage by a formidable wrought iron grille cutting it in two equal parts. On either side of this barrier certain noble lords, their armour covered with emblazoned cloaks, their hat brims encircled with precious stones.

On the right, King Edward IV of England, prematurely paunchy, his once beautiful face already marred by the stigmata of debauchery. On the left, the King of France . . . or, rather two Kings of France, dressed exactly alike in velvet embroidered with gold thread and black hats decorated with gems: for, carrying prudence to the limit, Louis XI has asked his crony Philip de Commines to wear exactly the same clothes as himself. Ever since the death of John the Fearless at Montereau, bridges had been considered unhealthy places for the mighty.

At an agreed signal the two kings moved towards each other like dancers beginning a movement in a ballet; but dancers in a state of nervous anxiety. They met at the grille and there not only exchanged a thousand graceful compliments through the bars, but even kissed each other on the mouth. A Bible having been pushed with some difficulty under the lowest bar, both Kings swore to respect the conditions of the truce which they had sealed and which was to last for nine years. The Lady Elizabeth of York, daughter of the King and Elizabeth Woodville, was to marry the Dauphin Charles: she was to receive annually, '*pour se nourrir*' a sum equal to the revenue of Guyenne. The King of France was to pay his brother of England an indemnity of 75,000 gold crowns, in return for which Edward agreed to take himself and his knights home to England. Whether they liked it or not, the Dukes of Burgundy and Brittany were included in the truce.

There was one more clause, almost a sentimental one: as a good kinsman Louis XI would pay ransom for his cousin, Margaret of Anjou, who had been a prisoner in the Tower of London for four years. The prisoner having renounced her jointure and all claims whatever on England, Edward agreed to return her to her family for 50,000 crowns.

The victor in the War of the Roses could hardly contain himself for joy. This expedition without a battle, which had cost him the lives of only three men, brought him more than Hexham, Towton and Tewkesbury together. It had put him in a position to give his wife, his family and his mistresses everything they wanted without vexing his followers with demands for money. The Lords fully shared the King's satisfaction: they were returning home gorged with good wine, gold chains, and pensions, blessing good King Louis who was such a skinflint with his own people, so prodigal when it came to dealing with his adversaries.

Such was the conclusion of a farce in which everyone involved thought he was duping the others, and all were dupes. The Constable de Saint-Pol who had supposed himself to be pulling all the strings in this business, found himself so entangled in them that in the end it cost him his life.

Saint-Pol had built up his position and his prodigious fortune in twelve years by selling his two masters to each other alternately: the King of France to the Duke of Burgundy, and the Duke of Burgundy to the King of France. Then came the great day when he conceived his masterpiece: he would sell both rogues together to a third rascal.

Charles of Burgundy having been called first 'the Brave' and then 'the Terrible' was now only 'the Rash'. At the moment when his ambition attained the most visionary heights, his luck abandoned him. He had just come badly out of a clash with Louis XI; his agents were being massacred in Alsace; for nine months he had been marking time outside the small town of Neuss on which he was wasting the flower of his armies and his empire's reserves. Far from heeding these warnings, he was preparing to attack Lorraine, the Swiss, and several German states. Saint-Pol persuaded him that he would do well to avoid being taken in the rear; he should neutralize his French rival by provoking an English invasion. Charles harkened to the tempter, and called in his brother-in-law.

The Constable promised all things to all men: to King Louis that he would stop the invader, to Edward IV several ports in Normandy and the Somme towns; to Charles a royal crown to be fashioned from the remnants of the two kingdoms.

Louis XI was the only one of the three who was not caught in the trap. He had Eu and Saint-Valery, which

Saint-Pol was responsible for defending, burnt; he changed all the Picard garrisons; and scorched the earth along the line of the enemy's advance.

Edward IV expected an easy war, expected the English royal standard to be hoisted on castle after castle at the mere tidings of his approach. This conviction, and the hope of loot, had alone persuaded him to leave the feasting and wenching which, for four years, had been his relaxation from the cares of state. Great was his rage upon being disappointed in both respects. Charles the Rash refused to open to him the towns of his Duchy, forcing him to sleep under the stars and depriving him of the chance to amuse himself with Flemish girls for a change. Added to which, the Burgundian was never in the same place or of the same mind for a day at a time, but always off after some new vagary, or chasing a new whim. He quickly lost interest in his ally and went off to cope with business in Lorraine.

Louis XI seized his chance. A common servant with a ready wit,* Mérichon by name, contrived to make his way into the English camp. There he threw off his villein's clothes and revealed the tunic of a herald of the French Crown. He was bringing Edward some attractive propositions.

Louis knew that there were two English weaknesses which he could play upon: the Queen's ambition and the cupidity of the English lords. Officially, he offered to marry the Dauphin to Elizabeth of York; unofficially, rich gifts to Edward's councillors. Edward and his councillors took his bait: the bargain was a good one—good coined gold instead of the uncertain glory of battles.

Once again France's royal usurer had pulled off a wonderful stroke of business. At a cost of one hundred and twenty-five thousand crowns, he rid France of the English, left Charles the Rash to the tender mercies of

* *'gentil esprit'*; the implication may be that he had a superior mind.

Swiss pikes, bought Saint-Pol's head for the executioner, and acquired a first class mortgage on the House of Anjou.

For four and a half years the woman whose cradle had been emblazoned with the arms of Anjou, Sicily and Lorraine, who had been the most admired princess of her day, and whom the Archbishop of Canterbury had crowned Queen of England, had been vegetating in one of the state prisons in the Tower of London.

Margaret was doubly a prisoner in that place, a prisoner not only of its locks but of her own grief, her mourning which was, from time to time, deepened by news of yet another loss: there was the death of Nicholas of Anjou, her nephew and John of Calabria's only heir; then that of her uncle Charles of Maine; Louis XI's iniquitous proceedings against King René, the ruin of the family she was born into following on that of the family she had married into.

Only her father still survived out of all the people she had loved. From Yolande of Aragon to the young prince Nicholas—who was probably poisoned just before his projected marriage to Marie of Burgundy, they formed a tragic avenue of ghosts now, extending away into the past: Isabel of Lorraine, Suffolk, the four Somersets, Owen Tudor, Charles VII, Brézé, John of Calabria, Henry VI, the Prince of Wales—ghosts and only ghosts filled the Queen's mind.

Then one day she was told that Louis XI was paying her ransom and that she would be restored to freedom and her own country. What transports of joy would, in the past, have been hers upon hearing such news. And with what wild happiness she would once again set out to seek her fortune. But not now; the murders of her son had killed the heroic spirit in her. Passive and contemptuous she accompanied Thomas Montgomery, charged by Edward with the duty of conveying her back to France. Towards the end of January 1476 she left for ever the cruel land of England where she had suffered every martyrdom of heart and mind that a woman can be called upon to endure.

She landed in Dieppe and from there travelled to Rouen. There envoys from the French King, Jean d'Hagest, captain of Rouen, and Jean Raguier, Receiver General of Normandy, awaited her. Their business was to receive her from her warders and also to make her pay without delay the debt of gratitude which she had contracted towards her cousin. Margaret had not been left in ignorance of what her freedom would cost her: had her son been still alive she would doubtless have argued, tried to defend herself. But what did this world's goods matter to her now?

Louis XI, greedy as ever to add more provinces to France, was keeping an anxious eye on the Angevins' territory. Lorraine had slipped through his fingers, having unanimously chosen as its Duke René of Vaudemont, the son of Ferry and Yolande, whose grandfather had already given him the Barrois. But the King had every intention of getting his hands on Maine and Anjou which had so foolishly been alienated by John the Good in favour of his second son. Provence had never belonged to the Domaine; but Louis nevertheless intended also to annex that beautiful province which had formerly belonged to the Empire.

Very soon Louis' patience became exhausted at having to wait for his uncle, still a hale and hearty man at sixty-six, to die. Pretending to believe an invented story that René had made a will leaving his lands to the Duke of Burgundy, he seized Anjou and immediately changed its constitutional state from feudal to monarchic centralization. At the same time Louis prosecuted the old King *in absentia*, in the Court of Peers. Despite the axiom that might is right, such a trial was not likely to get him very far; what Louis needed was a legal right to the succession when René died.

Since Yolande's children renounced their claim to the patrimony in exchange for the Barrois and Lorraine, René's heirs were reduced in number to only two— Margaret, and Charles of Maine's son, who was unable to father children. Louis XI required Margaret to make him a pre-emptive donation of her right which would enable him to inherit in her place when René died.

The unfortunate Queen had already lost her jointure, her kingdom and even her title. Now she was being obliged to strip herself of her last chance of any kind of future, and to bury herself at forty-six in the common living grave of people without resources, without family and without a roof. She did not even try to defend herself. When absolutely nothing remained to her, perhaps they would stop persecuting her. On 29 January 1476 she signed a renunciation which transferred to Louis XI all the claim she would, through René, eventually have to Lorraine, the Barrois, Anjou and Provence: those four provinces were specifically named in the document which opens with a phrase truly poignant in its simplicity: *Ego, Margarita, olim in regno Angliae maritata* . . . I, Margaret, formerly married in the Kingdom of England . . . what a welter of battles, crime, heroic acts and ordeals were there reduced to those seven words of Latin.

Several historians have denied that this cession had any significance. But Louis' haste in the business, the urgency with which he had it signed, and his promptness in making use of it are more than sufficient proof that they are at fault. For the moment he had the precious parchment in his hands his attitude to his uncle suddenly changed: he sent conciliatory proposals to Aix.

René agreed to swear an oath on the cross of Saint-Laud that he would never attempt any undertaking against France, and he then went to Lyon to confer with Louis XI. The King displayed his most tractable side and was gentle and even affectionate. After lengthy negotiations he consented to restore Anjou but only on condition that his reforms were retained, notably the Angers *Mairie*, one of his creations. In exchange, René definitively put aside his grandson, René of Vaudemont, from the succession to Anjou and Provence and recognized his nephew, Charles II of Maine as his sole heir. And by a secret convention of 25 May 1476, Charles undertook to bequeath his estate to the King of France.

This agreement was made possible only by the Queen of England's withdrawal of her claims. Yet she seemed meanwhile to have been quite forgotten. Margaret, who had thus enriched the kingdom with three provinces, and those among the most opulent of modern France, was herself in some danger of dying of starvation.

Some have believed that she went to live with René and played Antigone to the old man who like her had so much to bear. But it was certainly not so.

The father and his daughter had temperaments too opposed to be of any real comfort to each other. A calm fatalism, and a highly developed power of forgetting enabled the old King to suffer 'the slings and arrows of outrageous fortune' without flinching. When the Neapolitans rose against him he exiled himself from Naples. Did they try to pick a quarrel with him over Lorraine? He abandoned it to his children. Did the King of France take Anjou away from him? René withdrew to Provence. The deaths of John of Calabria and Nicholas had been cruel blows; but René still had his best consolation, his darling shepherdess Jeanne de Laval.

Margaret would certainly not have agreed to distract his mind and heart from his grief, among his pastoral amusements. She begged him to give her the castle called Reculée; he did so and also paid her a modest pension which enabled her to lead a more or less cheese-paring existence. Reculée was near Angers and very prettily sited.

From the height of a famous gallery which the artist-King had taken pleasure in embellishing with his own paintings, there was a pleasing view of a countryside nicely ordered with that easy, impressive grace which is so specifically French. There Margaret lived several contemplative years. Unlike so many of her contemporaries she did not take refuge in passionate devoutness. Her piety seems never to have been very fervent; and the greatness of her unhappiness, far from bringing her nearer to God, seems rather to have driven her from Him. Nor did the Queen seek distraction or relief in those literary occupations which her education and her informed mind would have made a possible refuge. She had the memory of her dead: that was enough.

At the end of the year 1479 she received as guests a number of exiled Lancastrian noblemen who came to her as to an object of pilgrimage. Thus she heard the scandalous gossip of Edward IV's court, heard of Anne Neville's monstrous marriage with Richard, Duke of Gloucester, of Clarence's arrest and mysterious death—the Prince, it was rumoured, had been drowned in a butt of Malmsey wine.

Margaret was not to know the final outcome of the terrible war which she herself had for so long stirred up and waged; she was not to see Gloucester avenge his own victims by exterminating the House of York to clear his way to the throne; never to witness the prodigious reversal of fortune which, after thirty years of reverses, gave final victory to Lancaster in the person of Henry Tudor. But perhaps that ignorance was a blessing. As a mother she would have been too cruelly tried by the spectacle of a miracle from which the Prince of Wales could not benefit.

And her trials were still not over.

On 10 July 1480 King René died at seventy-one years of age. In his *Chronicle*, Bourdigne gives him the noblest epitaph that any monarch could have or hope for:

No prince ever loved his subjects as he loved his, nor was in like manner better loved and well-wished than he was by them.

According to the conventions entered into, the whole heritage fell to Charles II of Maine; the shadow of Louis XI was lengthening across the Angevin provinces. To her grief as a daughter Margaret now had to add the most humiliating of anxieties: who, thenceforth would pay that pension which was all that remained between her and utter poverty?

Three weeks after René's death she wrote to the Sieur de Bouchage, one of the old King's councillors who had been won over by Louis XI, and who had contributed so much to establishing the French in Provence. Not even Margaret's worst enemy could have read with indifference a letter in which the haughtiest of Queens was reduced to humbly soliciting the benevolence of a financier.

*Monsieur de Bouchage*, I commend myself to you as much as I can. The King has made known to the town of Angers that the King of Sicily, *Monseigneur* my father, is gone to God. I am writing to him that it may please him to take my poor case, in the matter of what can and should belong to me, into his hands to do with it according to his good will and pleasure, and still keep me in his good grace and love, in which I pray you to be good enough to maintain me always. And [I commend you] to God, Monsieur de Bouchage, may he give you all that you wish. Written at Reculée-les-Angiers, the first day of August 1480.

Margaret.

Louis XI's 'good will and pleasure' was, first and foremost, to extort from the poor woman anything she still had to give. The King forced her to confirm her donation of 1476; and then to proceed at law against her sister Yolande for resignation of her right to the Barrois which the insatiable monarch wanted, despite his promises, to get his hands on. In the hope of being given the means to live the rest of her life honourably, Margaret gave way to him. But she was not granted even the poor satisfaction of being able, by her compliance, to provide for her needs. Once Louis believed that nothing more was to be got out of her, he left her penniless. She had to leave Reculée, and it looked as if the world was to be treated to the spectacle of a Queen of England begging her bread at the roadside.

All that saved her from that last mortification was the feudal chivalry of an Angevin country gentleman, Francis Vignolles, lord of Morains. Moved by compassion he offered the daughter of his liege lord hospitality in his castle of Dampierre: and Dampierre was to be Margaret's last home.

Dampierre stands beside and overlooks the Loire about three miles from Saumur. At that point in its course the river winds placidly in broad meanderings so that the horizons are pleasing minglings of water and trees. Are we to suppose that this peaceful harmony brought the exile from the great world a measure of spiritual comfort? Rather must it often have been a torture—that limpid tranquil silence—to an ear attuned to the tumult of battle and the clamour of revolution. So great and apparent was her distress that it became proverbial among the good people of the countryside. Yet her dignity remained intact and the very few visitors she received left her presence as overcome with admiration as the men who had courted her smile when she was a girl of twenty. Under the coarse dress which was all she could afford, the Queen was still a queen.

On 19 December 1481 it was Charles of Maine's turn to join his ancestors and with indifference Margaret signed a will in Louis XI's favour. The union of France, Maine, Anjou and Provence was accomplished, and the Valois became claimants to the throne of the Two Sicilies.

Meanwhile the woman who had thus superlatively endowed her country was dying, ignored, and perhaps forgotten. In August 1482 she suddenly became very feeble: still Margaret of Anjou, however, she was determined to meet the last grim enemy as she had met all the others—with the proud stoicism which no reverse could disturb: without Court, without servants, kinless and friendless, lying in threadbare sheets, worn out, burnt out, the Queen died as she had lived, nobly true to herself; died of old age—at fifty-two.

A modest tomb was hastily contrived for her: neither Henry VII when he became the autocrat of England, nor Francis I after Marignano so much as thought of paying a moment's respect to the shade, the memory of the woman to whom they owed their power and their glory. And English schoolchildren were taught to hate her as the wicked Frenchwoman, and never knew that she was the most beautiful, as she was the unhappiest of women; as a Queen heroic, as a mother, sublime.

THE END

Kings of France

House of Valois and Anjou

John II (the Good) 1319–64, King of France 1350,
married 1332, Bonne of Luxemburg, who died 1349, 7 children

Charles V (the Wise) 1337–80, King of France 1364,
married 1350 Joanna de Bourbon, 1338–78, 3 children

Charles VI 1368–1422, King of France 1380,
married 1385 Isabeau of Bavaria, 1370–1435, 12 children

Isabel 1389–1409
married 1395 Richard II
King of England, died 1399
without issue

Catherine 1400–38
married (1) 1420 Henry V
King of England,
who died 1422 married (2)
1422 Owen Tudor

Edmond Tudor
died 1456, married
Margaret Beaufort, who
died 1509

Henry VII Tudor, 1456–1509
King of England 1485
(see table 3)

Charles VII, 1403–61,
King of France, 1422
married 1422
Marie of Anjou
daughter of Louis II,
King of Sicily 1404–63,
14 children

Louis XI, 1423–83,
King of France 1461,
married 1436 (1)
Margaret of Scotland
1418–44, who died
without issue
(2) Charlotte of Savoy,
3 children

Henry VI, King of England,
born 1421; crowned King
of France 1431, died 1471
married Margaret of Anjou
(see right column),
who died 1482

Edward of Lancaster,
Prince of Wales, 1453–72,
married 1470 Anne Neville,
daughter of the
Earl of Warwick (see table 3)

Louis I, Duke of Anjou 1339–84,
adopted by Joanna I, Queen of Sicily 1380,
King of Naples, Sicily and Jerusalem in 1382,
married 1360, Marie, Countess of Guise, daughter
of Charles of Blois, who died 1404

Louis II of Anjou, 1377–1417, King of Sicily 1384,
married 1400 Yolande of Aragon, who died 1442, 5 children

Marie of Anjou
1404–63, married
1422 Charles VII,
(see left column)

Louis III of Anjou
1403–34 titulary
King of Sicily 1421
married 1431
Margaret of Savoy,
no issue

René of Anjou
1408–80, Duke of
Lorraine and Bar,
Count of Provence,
adopted by Joanna II
of Naples, 1434
Duke of Anjou,
King of Sicily, 1435 King
of Naples, married (1)
Isabel of Lorraine,
who died 1453,
(2) 1454 Jeanne de
Laval, who died 1498,
3 children from
1st marriage

John II of Anjou 1424–70,
Duke of Calabria 1453,
married 1441 Marie
of Bourbon, who died 1488

Nicholas of Anjou
1448–73, Duke of
Lorraine in 1470,
died unmarried

Yolande of Anjou
1428–83, Duchess of
Lorraine 1473,
married 1445 Ferry
de Vaudémont, who
died in 1470, 4 children

René II, Duke of
Lorraine, 1451–1508

Margaret of Anjou
1430–82, married 1446
Henry VI, King of England,
who died 1471
(see left column)

Charles of Anjou,
Count of Maine
1414–72,
married Isabeau
of Luxembourg

Charles II of Anjou,
Count of Maine &
Provence 1436–87,
married Jeanne of
Vaudémont-Lorraine
1448–80

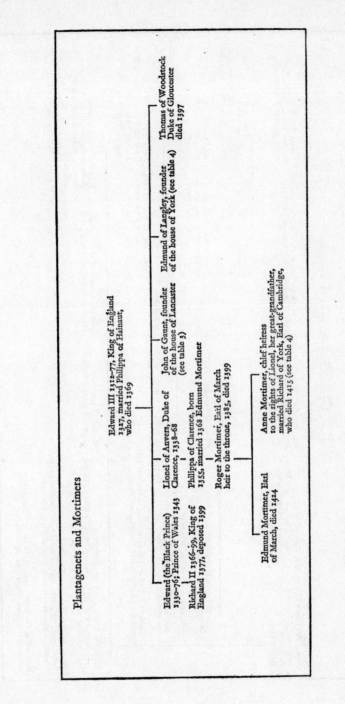

Plantagenets and Mortimers

# House of Lancaster (Red Rose)

John of Gaunt, 1340–99,
3rd son of Edward III, Duke of Lancaster, married 3 times

**Henry IV** (Henry Bolingbroke, Duke of Lancaster,
1366–1413) King of England 1399, married (1) 1380 Mary
de Bohun, who died 1394: (2) Joanna of Navarre, who
died in 1437

John Beaufort, Earl of Somerset,
died 1410, married Margaret Holand

**Henry Beaufort, Bishop of Lincoln,
Cardinal of Winchester, died 1447**

Joanna Beaufort
married Ralph Neville, Earl
of Westmoreland, died 1440

Richard Neville, Earl of
Salisbury, died 1461

**Richard Neville, Earl
of Warwick** (the Kingmaker)
died 1471, married Anne
Beauchamp

Cicely Neville
died 1495, married Richard,
Duke of York, who died 1460

Edward IV
King of England
1442–83,
(see table 4)

John Beaufort, Earl then Duke
of Somerset, died 1444

**Edmund Beaufort, 2nd Duke of
Somerset, died 1455** married Eleanor
Beauchamp

Isabel 1451–76, married 1469
George, Duke of Clarence
(see table 4)

**Anne, married (1) 1470
Edward, Prince of Wales,** (table 1)
(2) 1471 Richard III,
King of England (table 4)

Margaret Beaufort, and heiress of
the Lancasters, died 1509. Married
Edmund Tudor, Earl of Richmond
(see table 1)

**Edmund Beaufort,
4th Duke of Somerset,
died 1471**

**Henry Beaufort, 3rd
Duke of Somerset, died 1463**

Henry VII Tudor 1456–1509, King of England 1485,
married Elizabeth of York 1486 (see table 4)

Thomas of Lancaster,
Duke of Clarence, died 1421

John of Lancaster, Duke of Bedford,
Regent of France, died 1435

**Humphrey of Lancaster,
Duke of Gloucester, Lord
Protector & Lord Chamberlain
died 1446**

**Henry V,** 1388–1422, King of England
1413, Regent of France 1420, married Catherine of Valois
1420 (see table 1)

**Henry VI** 1421–71, King of England 1422, King of
France 1431, dethroned 1461, restored 1470, dethroned 1471.
Married Margaret of Anjou, who died 1482 (see table 1)

**Edward of Lancaster,** 1453–71, Prince of Wales 1454,
married 1470, Anne Neville (see right column)

# House of York (White Rose)

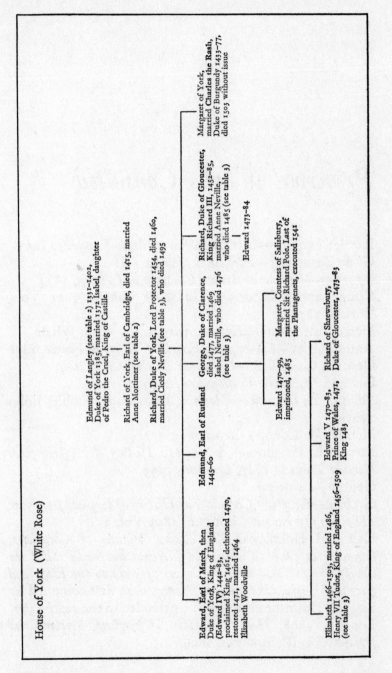

Edmund of Langley (see table 2) 1331-1402, Duke of York 1385, married 1372 Isabel, daughter of Pedro the Cruel, King of Castile

Richard of York, Earl of Cambridge, died 1415, married Anne Mortimer (see table 2)

Richard, Duke of York, Lord Protector 1454, died 1460, married Cicely Neville (see table 3), who died 1495

Edward, Earl of March, then Duke of York (Edward IV) 1442-83, proclaimed King 1461, dethroned 1470, restored 1471, married 1464 Elizabeth Woodville

Edmund, Earl of Rutland 1445-60

George, Duke of Clarence, died 1477, married 1469 Isabel Neville, who died 1476 (see table 3)

Richard, Duke of Gloucester, King Richard III, 1452-85, married Anne Neville, who died 1485 (see table 3)

Margaret of York, married Charles the Rash, Duke of Burgundy 1433-77, died 1503 without issue

Elizabeth 1466-1503, married 1486, Henry VII Tudor, King of England 1456-1509 (see table 3)

Edward V 1470-83, Prince of Wales, 1471, King 1483

Richard of Shrewsbury, Duke of Gloucester, 1473-83

Edward 1470-99, imprisoned 1485

Margaret, Countess of Salisbury, married Sir Richard Pole. Last of the Plantagenets, executed 1541

Edward 1473-84

# Principal Works Consulted

Barbier-Langlois—Article in *Revue Anglo-Française*, 1837
G. de Beaucourt—*Histoire de Charles VII*
Bourcier—Article in *Revue Historique de l'Anjou*, 1874
César Cantu—*Documenti alla Storia Universale*, 11 Vols,
Torino, 1872
Pierre Champion—*Louis XI*, 1929, trans W. S. Whale
Jean Chartier—*Chronique de Charles VII, roi de France*, 1858
Georges Chastellain—*Chronique des choses de ce temps*
Georges Cheruel—*Dictionnaire historique*
Philippe de Comines—*Memoirs*, trans A. R. Scoble, Bohn
1901–4
Mathieu de Coucy—*Chronique*
Samuel R. Gardiner—*A Student's History of England from
Earliest Times to 1885*, London, 1893
George—*Chronique*
Grafton—*Grafton's Chronicle; or History of England from year
1189 to 1558 inclusive*, London, 1809 Vol. 2
Hall and Holinshead—*The Third Volume of Chronicles,
Beginning at Duke William the Norman commonlie called the
Conqueror, and descending by degrees of years to the Kings and
Queens of England in their orderlie successions*, first compiled by
Raphael Holinshead and by him extended to the yeare 1577,
London. 1808, *Hall's Chronicles of England, Scotland and
Ireland* Vol. III, London, 1809

Mary Ann Hookham—*The Life and Times of Margaret of Anjou*, London, 1872

André Joubert—'Les invasions anglaises en Anjou aux XIV$^e$ et XV$^e$ siecles', Article in *Revue Historique et archéologique du Maine*

Lecoy de Lamarche—*Le Roi René*, Paris ,1875

Jules Michelet—*History of France*, 2 Vols, London, 1844, trans. G. H. Smith

Enguerrand de Monstrelet—*Chronicles of Monstrelet*, trans. T. Johnes, London, 1840

Emile Montegut—Notes and appendices to the translation of Shakespeare's *Henry V* and *Henry VI* parts I, II, and III

Jean Petithuguenin—*La Vie Tragique de Marguerite d'Anjou*

J. J. S. Roy—*Histoire de Marguerite d'Anjou*, Tours, 1872

Thomas Rymer—*Foedera*, London, 1704-32

Agnes Strickland—*The Lives of the Queens of England*, 6 Vols. London, 1877

Sharon Turner—*History of England*, London, 1825

Vallet de Viriville—*Histoire de Charles VII*, Paris, 1863-5